Writing Language, Culture, and Development:
Africa Vs Asia
Volume 1

Edited by:
Tendai Rinos Mwanaka
Upal Deb
Wanjohi wa Makokha

Mwanaka Media and Publishing Pvt Ltd,
Chitungwiza Zimbabwe
*
Creativity, Wisdom and Beauty

i

Publisher:

Mmap

Mwanaka Media and Publishing Pvt Ltd

24 Svosve Road, Zengeza 1

Chitungwiza Zimbabwe

mwanaka@yahoo.com

https//mwanakamediaandpublishing.weebly.com

Distributed in and outside N. America by African Books Collective

orders@africanbookscollective.com

www.africanbookscollective.com

ISBN: 978-0-7974-8493-1

EAN: 9780797484931

DISCLAIMER

All views expressed in this publication are those of the author and do not necessarily reflect the views of *Mmap*.

Contents

Notes on contibutors...x-ix
Introduction...xx-xxiii
Nonfictions...1-26

INTRODUCTION TO INTERNATIONAL STUDIES
(RELATIONS)IN WEST AFRICA UP TO 1500: CHINESE,
EUROPEAN AND ARAB CONNECTIONS: *Lemuel Ekedegwa Odeh*
(Nigeria)
RHINO-CIDE: *Jill Hedgecock (USA)*

Fictions...27-83

A DARK ENERGY, Chapter 11, a novel extract: *Tendai Rinos*
Mwanaka (Zimbabwe)
Prologue: Servants of the Rice, A novel extract: *Audrey McCombs*
(USA):
Okwu n'eso Akuko: Odibo Osikapa: *Audrey McCombs (translation into*
Igbo by Gabriel Egboluche)
His eyes were blue: *Ian Broinowski (Australia)*
Idonsashudi*: Ian Broinowski (translation into Hausa by Abdulrahman.S.*
Waziri and Mustapha Tanko)
PRESSURE POINT: *Lee Ray Khan (Nepal)*
दबाबपोष्ट: *Lee Ray Khan(translation into Nepelese by Lee Ray Khan)*
Reminiscences: *Mona Lisa Jena (India)*
SCARLET: *Ayo Oyeku (Nigeria)*

Poetry...84-247

人生之: *Changming Yuan (China/ Canada)*

Water of Life: *Changming Yuan (translation from Chinese by Changming Yuan)*

思想猎人: *Changming Yuan (China/Canada)*

Thought Hunting: *Changming Yuan (translation from Chinese by Changming Yuan)*

追求: *Changming Yuan (China/Canada)*

Pursuing: *Changming Yuan (translation from Chinese by Changming Yuan)*

图腾柱: *Tao Zhijian (China/Canada)*

The Totem Pole: *Tao Zhijian (ttranslation from Chinese by Tao Zhijian)*

白金城市: Hongri Yuan (China)

Platinum City: Hongri Yuan *(Translation from Chinese by Manu Mangattu)*

There Were Moments: *Emily Achieng' (Kenya/South Korea)*

그랬던 적이 있었다.: *Emily Achieng' (translation into Korean by 이의영):*

Былимоменты: *Emily Achieng' (translation into Russian by Aizhan)*

Uncertainty: *Emily Achieng' (Kenya/South Korea)*

Languages: *Emily Achieng' (Kenya/South Korea)*

DISPATCH FROM HORIZON: *Wanjohi wa Makokha (Kenya)*

DAUGHTER OF THE LAUNDRESS: *Wanjohi wa Makokha (Kenya)*

OF HOMELAND AMIDST BEYOND: *Wanjohi wa Makokha (Kenya)*

a solitary maiden stands: *Archie Swanson (South Africa)*

孤高の少女が立つ: *Archie Swanson (translation into Japanese by Fumio Ueno)*

ombak indah rain: *Archie Swanson (South Africa)*

ombak indah rain: *Archie Swanson (translation into Japanese by Fumio Ueno)*

Gwalior: *Amitabh Mitra (South Africa)*

Gwalior: *Amitabh Mitra (translation into Japanese by Fumio Ueno)*

Jacob in Hebron: *Christina A Lee (Australia/Italy)*

Yakobo wekuHeberoni: *Christina A. Lee (translation into Shona by Tendai Rinos Mwanaka)*

strange heights: *Christina A Lee (Australia/Italy)*

Makomo emashiripiti: *Christina A Lee (translation into Shona by Tendai Rinos Mwanaka)*

African Heirloom: *Lind Grant-Oyeye (Nigeria/Canada)*

Afrika Chishongedzo: *Lind Grant-Oyeye (translation into Shona by Tendai Rinos Mwanaka)*

Mourning: *Lind Grant-Oyeye (Nigeria/Canada)*

Good bye Manaima: *Lind Grant-Oyeye (Nigeria/Canada)*

Wako wekutumbura: *Gumisai Nyoni (Zimbabwe)*

For yours that you gave birth to: *Gumisai Nyoni (translation from Shona by Tendai Rinos Mwanaka)*

Sevai Muto: *Gumisai Nyoni (Zimbabwe)*

Have its soup: *Gumisai Nyoni (translation from Shona by Tendai Rinos Mwanaka)*

Dundundu Nhando: *Gumisai Nyoni (Zimbabwe)*

Fake Pride: *Gumisai Nyoni (translation from Shona by Tendai Rinos Mwanaka)*

The precision of MEASUREMENT!: *Poornima Laxmeshwar (India)*

OMIA Kpakpa: *Poornima Laxmeshwar (translation into Idoma by Lemuel Ekedegwa Odeh)*

Tales of tequila: *Poornima Laxmeshwar (India)*

lab rats: *Rohith (India)*

makonzo emumba mesayenze: *Rohith (translation into Shona by Tendai Rinos Mwanaka)*

Hospital: *Rohith (India)*

Where I come from...who I am....: *Smeetha Bhoumik (India)*

Kwandakabva.... zvandiri....: *Smeetha Bhoumik (translation into Shona by Tendai Rinos Mwanaka)*

What I See: *Smeetha Bhoumik (India)*

How I Wonder!: *Smeetha Bhoumik (India)*

ONE WORLD: *Eniola Olaosebikan (Nigeria)*

Motherland chant: *Eniola Olaosebikan (Nigeria)*

أنشودة الوطن: *Eniola Olaosebikan (translation into Arabic by Fethi Sassi)*

For colored only?: *Eniola Olaosebikan (Nigeria)*

للمتلوّنين فقط ؟: *Eniola Olaosebikan (translation into Arabic by Fethi Sassi)*

Roots: *Vinita Agrawal (India)*

Midzi yedzinza: *Vinita Agrawal (translation into Shona by Tendai Rinos Mwanaka)*

Black Waters: *Vinita Agrawal (India)*

Writers Without Borders: *Vinita Agrawal (India)*

With This Pen: *Edward Dzonze (Zimbabwe)*

بهذا القلم : *Edward Dzonze (translation into Arabic by Fethi Sassi)*

Poetry Cookies: *Nalini Priyadarshni (India)*

Kashata za Ushairi: *Nalini Priyadarshi (translation into Kiswahili by Wanjohi wa Makokha)*

Love We Deserve: *Nalini Priyadarshni (India)*

Penzi Tustahililo: *Nalini Praiyadarshni (translation into Kiswahili by Kariuki wa Nyamu)*

Half Kiss: *Nalini Priyadarshni (India)*

Nusu Busu: *Nalini Priyadarshni (translation into Kiswahili by Kariuki wa Nyamu)*

OPELE: *NURENI Ibrahim (Nigeria)*

الخرز : *NURENI Ibrahim (translation into Arabic by Fethi Sassi)*

Portrait of the poet as young woman: *Chandramohan S (India)*

Picha Ya Malenga Kama Mwanamwali: *Chandramohan S (translation into Kiswahili by Kariuki wa Nyamu)*

THIRTEEN WAYS OF LOOKING AT A BLACK BURKINI: *Chandramohan S (India)*

NJIA KUMI NA TATU ZA KUTAZAMA BURKINI NYEUSI: *Chandramohan S (translation into Kiswahili by Kariuki wa Nyamu)*

Beef poem: *Chandramohan S (India)*

Shairi Nyama: *Chandramohan S (translation into Kiswahili by Kariuki wa Nyamu)*

ROBERT MUGABE STREET: *Phumulani Chipandambira (Zimbabwe):*

Ulayi U Robert Mugabe: *Phumulani Chipandambiri (translation into Idoma by Lemuel Ekedegwa Odeh)*

DAMBUDZO MARECHERA: *Phumulani Chipandambira (Zimbabwe):*

DAMBUDZO MARECHERA: *Phumulani Chipandambiri* *(translation from into Idoma by Lemuel Ekedegwa Odeh)*

A WRITER'S PEN: *Kariuki wa Nyamu (Kenya)*

AL{ALAMIN MARUBUCI: *Kariuki wa Nyamu (translation into Hausa by Abdulrahman.S. Waziri and Mustapha Tanko)*

If I may inquire…: *Kariuki wa Nyamu (Kenya)*

IN DA ZAN TAMBAYA: *Kariuki wa Nyamu (translation into Hausa by Abdulrahman.S. Waziri and Mustapha Tanko)*

Okot p'Bitek: *Kariuki wa Nyamu (Kenya)*

Okot p' Bitek: *Kariuki wa Nyamu (translation into Hausa by Abdulrahman.S. Waziri and Mustapha Tanko)*

Knowledge: *Rochelle Potkar (India)*

Maarifa: Rochelle Potkar *(translation into Kiswahili by Kariuki wa Nyamu)*

Syllabus: *Rochelle Potkar (India)*

Silabasi: *Rochelle Potkar (translation into Kiswahili by Kariuki wa Nyamu)*

Art of critiquing: *Rochelle Potkar (India)*

Sanaa ya uchambuzi: *Rochelle Potkar (translation into Kiswahili by Kariuki wa Nyamu, Kenya)*

BURRIED SECRECT: *Juma Brenda (Kenya)*

Sumasɛm: *Juma Brenda (translation into Akan Twi by Adjei Agyei Baah)*

A Dirge for the Delta: *Stephen Temitope David (Nigeria/ South Africa)*

BenabɔNwom MaDɛlta: *Stephen Temitope David (translation into Akan Twi by Adjei Agyei Baah)*

A Song for Independence: *Stephen Temitope David (Nigeria/ South Africa)*

FaahodieNwom: *Stephen Temitope (translation into Akan Twi by Adjei Agyei Baah)*

Silent Gods (For the kidnapped schoolgirls): *Stephen Temitope David (Nigeria/ South Africa)*

AbosomMmum: *Stephen Temitope David (translation into Akan Twi by Adjei Agyei Baah*

The Shape of the Heart: *Ryan Thorpe (China)*

Umbo la Roho: *Ryan Thorpe (translation into Kiswahili by Kariuki wa Nyamu)*

Walking to Work in Shanghai: *Ryan Thorpe (China)*
Kutembea hadi Kazini Jijini Shanghai: *Ryan Thorpe (translation into Kiswahili by Kariuki wa Nyamu)*
Untitled: *Daniel Ari (USA)*
Untitled: *Daniel Ari (translation into Japanese by Fumio Ueno)*
Benjamina Tree: *Shannon Hopkins (South Africa)*
Benjamina Tree: *Shannon Hopkins (translation into Japanese by Fumio Ueno)*
Freedom?: *Shannon Hopkins (South Africa)*
We are here: *Shannon Hopkins (South Africa)*
Hair things: *Tralone Lindiwe Khoza (South Africa)*
God I want to go to Ghana: *Tralone Lindiwe Khoza (South Africa)*

Plays..248-271

Lonely Bites: *Albert Jamae (Australia)*
Cizo Daya tilo: *Albert Jamae (translation into Hausa by Abdulrahman.S. Waziri and Mustapha Tanko)*
THE CHILD NO ONE LOVES (a playlet): *Solomon C.A. Awuzie (Nigeria):*

About editors

Tendai Rinos Mwanaka is a publisher, editor, mentor, writer, visual artist and musical artist with close to 20 books published which include among others, *Zimbolicious Poetry Anthologies (Anthology series of Zimbabwean poets), Playing To Love's Gallery (poetry book), Keys in the River (short stories novel), Voices from Exile (poetry book), Counting The Stars (poetry book),* and many more here: *http://www.africanbookscollective.com/authors-editors/tendai-rinos-mwanaka.*

viii

He writes in English and Shona. His work has appeared in over 400 journals and anthologies from over 27 countries. Work has been translated into Spanish, French and German.

Wanjohi wa Makokha (b.1979), is the sobriquet of Kenyan public intellectual JKS Makokha who is based at the Department of Literature and Institute of African Studies in Kenyatta University. Born in 1979 in Nairobi, raised in Eldoret and Bungoma, the poet has been shaped by various aspects of Kenyan cultures and environments. He obtained his elementary and secondary education from Muslim, Christian and Public schools. He holds tertiary papers from Kenyatta University, University of Leipzig and Free University of Berlin. This cross-cultural educational experience influences his vision and craft as an artist. The experience is sharpened by his private and public life that have seen him travel widely across Somalia, Uganda, Kenya, Zanzibar, Tanganyika, South Africa and Western Europe. He is the co-editor of several volumes of essays in literary criticism and theory such as: *Reading Contemporary African Literatures: Critical Perspectives (Amsterdam/New York, 2013); Border-Crossings: Narrative and Demarcation in Postcolonial Literatures (Heidelberg, 2012); Style in African Literatures (Amsterdam, 2012), and East African Literatures (Berlin, 2011)* among others. His poetry has been published in the *Atonal Poetry Review, African Writing, The Journal of New Poetry, Postcolonial Text, Stylus Poetry Journal and Kwani? 7*. Nest of Stones: Kenyan Narratives in Verse published by Langaa in 2010 is his debut book of verse. It revolves around the Kenya Election Crisis 2007-2008 and carries a foreword by the respected Kenyan poetess and scholar, Professor Micere Mugo.

Upal Deb is an Indian scholar and writer

Notes on Contributors

Emily Achieng' is from Nairobi, Kenya. She loves the stars, and better yet, looks at them more than most people do.

Vinita Agrawal, Author of three books of poetry, Vinita is a Mumbai based, award winning poet and writer. She is Editor Womaninc.com, an online platform that addresses gender issues. Recipient of the Gayatri GaMarsh Memorial Award for Literary Excellence, USA, 2015, her poems have appeared in *Asiancha, Constellations, The Fox Chase Review, Pea River Journal, Open Road Review, Stockholm Literary Review, Poetry Pacific, Mithila Review* and other journals. She was nominated for the Best of the Net Awards in 2011. She was awarded first prize in the Wordweavers Contest 2014, commendation prize in the All India Poetry Competition 2014 and won the 2014 Hour of Writes Contest thrice. Her poems have found a place in several anthologies. She contributes a monthly column on Asian Poets on the literary blog of the Hamline university, Saint Paul, USA. She has read at SAARC events, at the U.S. Consulate, at Delhi Poetree and at Cappucino Readings, Mumbai. She was featured in the transatlantic poetry broadcast. She can be reached at https://www.pw.org/content/vinita_agrawal and at www.vinitawords.com

Daniel Ari writes, publishes, performs and teaches poetry. This has grown out of his lifelong sense of play and wonder in relation to language and its deep, mysterious origins.

Solomon C. A. Awuzie is Solomon Awuzie's writing name. Solomon Awuzie obtained his B.A. degree from the Imo State University Owerri, his M.A. degree from the University of Ibadan and his PhD degree from the University of Port Harcourt. He is the author of *The Last Revolution*, and *The Born Again Devil*. In 2005, his short story, "Your Epistle", won the ANA-IMO / YOUNG

WRITERS CLUB prize for literature and in 2015 his children fiction, Oluyemi and the School Fee, came second at the ANA-IMO state literary competition. He teaches Literature at the Department of English, Edo University Iyamho.

Adjei Agyei-Baah is a language lecturer at the University of Ghana School of Distance Education, Kumasi Campus and author of two haiku books: *AFRIKU (Red Moon Press, 2016)* and *Ghana 21 Haiku (Mamba Africa Press, 2017)* and winner of several international awards. He is the co-founder of Africa Haiku Network (AHN) and as well doubles as the co-editor of Mamba Journal, Africa's first international haiku journal, and champions "Afriku", a nativized and avant-garde form of the Japanese haiku poetry in Africa and other places of the world.

Smeetha Bhoumik is an artist and a poet, working with traditional and new media, bringing the two together in interesting outcomes. Her main theme of work is the Universe Series, depicting the mysterious universe's star-forming regions, supernovae, galaxies, constellations and magic. She believes that we are all made of star dust and this oneness inspires her. Her work has shown in ten solo and more than forty group shows in India and abroad; and she is represented by the Global Art Agency. Her poetry speaks softly for the vulnerable. She is an alumnus of IIT Kharagpur, and Founder of Women Empowered-India (WE).

Ian Broinowski, PhD, MEd, BA(Soc Wk), BEc, Dip Teach, worked as an advanced skills teacher in children's services at TAFE Tasmania in Hobart, Australia for many years. Ian has a background in Economics, Social Work and Education. He has taught in a wide range of subjects in aged care, disability services, children's services, community and youth work. Ian's publications include *Child Care Social Policy and Economics, (1994) Creative Childcare Practice: Program design in early childhood, (2002)* and *Managing Children's Services 2004* as well as a range of professional journal articles.

Chandramohan S is an Indian English Dalit poet and literary critic based in Trivandrum, Kerala. He is part of P.K. Rosi foundation, a cultural collective (named after the legendary, pioneering Dalit actress) that seeks to de-marginalise Dalit-Bahujans. His first collection of poems titled *Warscape Verses* was published in May 2014. His second collection of poems is titled *Letters to Namdeo Dhasal* is forthcoming and few of his poems have been used at many protest sites. He has been anthologized in *LAND: an anthology of Indo-Australian poetry (Edited by Rob Harle)* and *40 poets under 40 (Edited by Nabina Das and Semeen Ali)*. He was instrumental in organizing in literary meets of English poets of Kerala for Ayyappa Panicker foundation and for Kritya Poetry festival.

Phumulani Chipandambira is a Zimbabwean freelance writer. He likes reading and writing poetry and short stories. He has been published in various local magazines and newspapers.

Stephen Temitope David is a Ph.D candidate in Stellenbosch University, South Africa. He is a performance poet who relies on African griot tradition for muse. He is a Nigerian.

Edward X. Dzonze's poetry seeks to capture the African panorama with minimal prejudice. His hand cannot be mistaken; it is famed for its pan-African eloquence and the profundity thereof-Born on the 4th of June 1989 in Mutoko, where he did his primary education. Edward X. Dzonze is a Zimbabwean born writer. He attended Mufakose 1 High School in Harare. Dzonze, a.k.a NRS(Nameles Radio Station) in the Spoken word circles, has published two poetry collections to date; *Many Truths Told at Once (Royalty Publishing USA, 2015)* and *Wisdom Speaks (Royalty Publishing USA,2016)* .He also co-edited the *Zimbolicious poetry anthology (Royalty Publishing USA, 2016)*. His other poetry has also been featured in; *World Peace poetry anthology (India, 2013)*, *We are One (Diaspora Publishers, UK, 2014)*, *Best New African Poets 2015 Anthology* , *Best New African Poets 2016 Anthology* and *Zimbolicious poetry anthology* respectively.

Dzonze a.k.a NRS is a full time writer. He lives in Harare's high density Surbub of Budiriro with his wife and two children.

Yugo Gabriel Egboluche is a graduate of Geography from the University of Nigeria, Nsukka. He writes from Anambra State, Nigeria where he works as a Development Practitioner. Together with poetry, he does fiction, non-fiction, screenwriting and copywriting. His works have been published in the *Kalahari Review, Praxis Magazine Online, Words, Rhyme & Rhythm* and his stories translated into film. His short stories have been published in *Experimental Writing, Volume 1, Africa vs Latin American anthology* and other webzines. He has also co-authored and edited more than two community development texts and guidebooks.

Jill Hedgecock has a Master's Degree in Environmental Management. She is a freelance writer who became aware about the devastating impact of poaching on rhino populations during a visit to South Africa. Jill is working on a novel to illuminate the complex causes of rhino poaching. Her article on the plight of the rhino appeared in May 2016 (http://www.diablogazette.com/issues/may-diablo-gazette/) and she gave a talk on this subject in June 2016 to the Mount Diablo Audubon Society. She is an active-status member of the Mount Diablo Branch of the California Writer's Club where she serves as their program chairperson.

Shannon Hopkins: is a writer living in Ballito on the KwaZulu-Natal North Coast of South Africa. She holds a BA degree in Fine Art and an Honours in English, and is currently studying for her Masters in English Literature at the University of KwaZulu-Natal, Durban. She has been published in a number of literary journals and anthologies. Hopkins is fascinated with writing as a means of creating understanding between different cultures and as a platform to explore, capture and remember issues of the times as well as that of personal experience.

NURENI Ibrahim is an award-winning poet based in Lagos, Nigeria. He has published poems both in local and international magazines/journals. His poem "Half of a Human Species" featured in Best New African Poets 2016 Anthology. He is one of the Joint Winners at the 2016 Calabar Poetry Festival Prize. He renders poetry both in verse and in performance. His poems "The Rhythm of Epiphany" and "Song of Violence" were dramatized at the Celebration of Black History Month, Ahmadu Bello University, Zaria and Purple Awareness Programme respectively. He is also a fanatic lover of Haiku.

Albert Jamae has been writing since 1998 in areas of stage, screen, and radio. His credits include a comedy webseries, a few short films, over a dozen plays for kids and adults, three full length school musicals and a series of online e-books comprising of around two hundred short scripts for actors and drama teachers. He's won awards for two of his one act plays and three national awards for writing radio commercials. He's currently developing a comedy TV series and writing his first teenage fiction novel.

Mona Lisa Jena was born in Odisha in 1964. She is the author of many books in various genres, including two collections of short stories, three books of poems and several volumes of translations. She has to her credit three collections of poems in Odia; Nisarga Dhwani and Ai Sabu Dhruba Muhurta and Nakshtra Devi. She has also written a novel *Nargis in Odia.* Her short stories are collected in *Indramalatira Shoka* and *Nilamadhabi.* Nargis is her latest novel. Ms Jena also wrote a biography of the noted Odia poet Ramakanta Rath besides translating and editing Dasuram's Script, a collection of contemporary Odia stories published by Harper Collins.She also translated Pratibha Ray's novel as *Citadel of love for Rupa* in 2015

Juma Brenda, is a Kenyan and a graduate of Theatre Arts and Film Technology from Kenyatta University and currently pursuing an MA in Film and Theatre Arts at Kenyatta University. She is a versatile artist -a published poet *Best 'New' African Poet 2016 Anthology*; a stage and screenwriter, Filmmaker, Actress and a makeup artist. She derives her passion and creativity from any form of art, be it literary, performing or visual arts. Her works revolve around social, political and economic commentaries.

Lee Ray Khan spent her girlhood in Australia but then travelled extensively in Europe and India. She now lives in a small village in Nepal. From time to time she sends out, without comment, stories by email.

Miss Tralone Lindiwe Khoza has a BA Communications degree from the University of Johannesburg (RAU) and a Post graduate Diploma in Marketing. She is a Marketing Specialist by profession, but writing is her first love. Her writing includes writing entertainment pieces for *All4Women, MUMSRU* a UK online magazine for single mothers, as well as the South Australian Fashion Magazine. Locally she writers for various online blogs and also writes regularly for Biz community on Marketing related articles. One of her poems, *Black Eagles* has recently being published in the *Best New African Poets 2016 Anthology*. She hopes to follow in the footsteps of many writers such as the late Dr. Maya Angelou.

Christina A Lee is originally from Melbourne, Australia. She is a part-time poet and art student who lives and works in Italy.

Poornima Laxmeshwar resides in the garden city Bangalore and works as a content writer for a living. Her poems have appeared in *Cold Noon, Vayavya, MuseIndia, Writers Asylum, The Aerogram, Stockholm Literary Review, Northeast Review, Brown Critique, Cafe Dissensus* amongst many others. Her haiku have found space in several magazines.

Manu Mangattu is Assistant Professor, Department of English, St George College, Aruvithura, India, more check his website www.mutemelodist.com

Audrey McCombs is currently a PhD student in theoretical ecology, earned her MFA in creative writing and environment. She served as the Creative Director for *Flyway: Journal of Writing and Environment* and her creative work has been published in *The Missing Slate, Sequestrum, The Mountain, Pithead Chapel, Earthspeak Magazine, Pay*

Attention: a River of Stones, and Beaches and *Parks from Monterey to Ventura.* She dreams of a three-year vow of silence, and a house empty of everything but blank walls upon which she may, finally, write down the code that animates our brute substance.

South African poet, **Amitabh Mitra** belongs to the city of Gwalior. An Orthopaedic Surgeon and an Emergency Medicine Expert in the black township of Mdantsane, Eastern Cape, he fuses his memories, the mind and lives in various planes.

Kariuki wa Nyamu is a passionate Kenyan poet, script writer, editor, translator, literary critic and educator. He obtained an Honours BA Education (Literature and English) from Makerere University, Uganda. His poetry won the National Book Trust of Uganda (NABOTU) Literary Awards 2007 and Makerere University Creative Writing Competition 2010. He is published in *A Thousand Voices Rising, Boda Boda Anthem and Other Poems, Best "New" African Poets 2015 Anthology, Experimental Writing: Africa Vs Latin America Anthology, Volume 1, Best "New" African Poets 2016 Anthology,* among others. He is presently pursuing a Master of Arts in Literature at Kenyatta University, Kenya.

Gumisai Nyoni was born in 1982, he went to Marowa Primary School, Nkululeko High School and Loreto High School. He completed BA Hons in Theatre Arts at University of Zimbabwe and a Post Graduate Diploma in Media Studies at UZ, again. He works as Chief Sub-Editor at Harare News.

Lemuel E. Odeh is a graduate of the Lagos State University Ojo- Lagos in B.A. History and International Studies, an M.sc International Relations and Strategic Studies and a Ph.D. in History from the Benue State University Makurdi. His area of research is Diplomatic History & International Economic Relations. He is currently a lecturer in the Department of History & International Studies, University of Ilorin, Nigeria. Dr Odeh has published extensively in the areas of economic history and international relations.

Eniola Olaosebikan is an active writer and a public speaker who currently shuffles between United Kingdom, United States and her home country Nigeria. She holds a master degree in International Business Management and asides writing and speaking, she works with specific organizations around the world to enable them realize their corporate goals.

Ayo Oyeku continues to fan the embers of his creative prowess, with over a decade contribution in the world of prose and poetry. His works have appeared in journals, publications and anthologies across the globe, including, *Illuminations (Celestial Arts, 2006); Fingernails across the Chalkboard (Third World Press, 2007); Miracle Literary Magazine (Miracle e-zinr, Issue 2, 2012); Stand Our Ground (Freedomseed Press, 2013); The Sky is Our Earth (Sankofa, 2015). According to Sources (Writers Project of Ghana, 2015),VINYL, Kalahari Review, AFREADA, Brittle Paper, Ebedi Review 2, and EXPERIMENTAL WRITING: Volume 1, Africa vs Latin America Anthology.* His heart-rending and inspiring debut novel, *Tears of the Lonely*, won the 2015 Ezenwa Ohaeta Award for Young Nigerian Novelists. And he was also shortlisted for the 2016 Golden Baobab Prize for Early Chapters. Currently, he is finishing up on his second novel.

Lind Grant-Oyeye is a widely published writer of African descent.

Rochelle Potkar is Author of *'The Arithmetic of Breasts and other stories', 'Four Degrees of Separation',* and *'Paper Asylum',* Rochelle Potkar is alumna of Iowa's International Writing Program (2015) and Charles Wallace Writer's fellowship, Stirling (2017). She is the winner of the 2016 Open Road Review story contest for *The leaves of the deodar.* Her story *Chit Mahal (The Enclave)* appears in The Best of Asian Short Stories. Her poems *Cellular: P.O.W.* and *Ground up* were shortlisted for awards. Her poem 'The girl from Lal Bazaar' was shortlisted for the Gregory O' Donoghue International Poetry Prize, 2018. She is editor of the Goan-Irish anthology, Goa: a garland of poems, with Gabriel Rosenstock, and co-founder of the Arcs-of-the-

Circle artists' residency program, Mumbai. https://rochellepotkar.com.

Nalini Priyadarshni is the author of *Doppelganger in My House* and co author of *Lines Across Oceans*. Her poems have appeared in numerous literary journals, podcasts and international anthologies including *Mad Swirl, Camel Saloon, Dukool, In-flight Magazine, Poetry Breakfast, The Riveter Review, The Open Road Review, Your One Phone Call, In Between Hangovers, Asian Signature* and *Yellow Chair Review*. Her poems and views on poetry and life have been featured on AIR (All India Radio) and FM radio. Her forthcoming publications include Silver Apples.

Rohith is a Medico from Government Medical College on Tirupati. He grew up in Anantapur. His poetry was published in various magazines like *The Sunflower Collective, Cafe Dissensus, Kritya, Raiot, The Brown Critique.*

Archie Swanson is a 61 year old Cape Town poet and surfer. His poems have been published in numerous anthologies and posted on a number of blogs. In 2016 three of his poems were translated into Spanish by Martín López-Vega, and published in the Spanish National newspaper, El Mundo. A poem also appears in *Experimental writing: Africa vs. Latin America, Volume 1.*

Dr. Ryan Thorpe teaches creative writing and literature at the University of Michigan-Shanghai Jiao Tong University Joint Institute. He is the fiction and poetry editor of The Shanghai Literary Review and manages a public workshop for anyone interested in creative writing. He writes columns for The Global Times, has published in numerous literary journals, and is currently working on a creative writing textbook. More information on his work can be found at www.rythorpe.com

Yuan Changming, nine-time Pushcart and one-time Best of Net nominee, published monographs on translation before moving out of China. With a Canadian PhD in English, Yuan currently edits *Poetry Pacific* with Allen Qing Yuan in Vancouver; credits include *Best of Best*

Canadian Poetry, BestNewPoemsOnline, New Coin, Rowayat, Threepenny Review and 1309 others across 39 countries.

Hongri Yuan, born in China in 1962, is a poet and philosopher interested particularly in creation. Representative works include *Platinum City, The City of Gold, Golden Paradise, Gold Sun* and *Golden Giant.* His poetry has been published in the UK, USA ,India ,New Zealand, Canada and Nigeria.

Tao Zhijian is a translator and scholar, with a doctorate from McGill and a membership with the Chinese Writers Association in Quebec, Canada. He has taught at several universities and worked also in the hydroelectric and hydrological fields. His published works include monograph *Drawing the Dragon: Western European Reinvention of China,* translations of the scholarly work *Bibliography Complex,* and art album Chung Siu Yau Series: the *Golden Age,* both from Chinese to English. Under his name are also four poetry collections in translation, entitled respectively *The Fortuities of a Shoe, A Line at Dawn, On the Shore Beyond,* and *Upon the Flower,* totalling some 320 poems. He has also published numerous critical essays, prose writings and poems, in both the English and Chinese languages, in scholarly journals, newspapers and literary magazines in China, Europe, the US as well as in Canada. Zhijian is presently engaged, as a translator, in the project of creating Chinese-English editions of two of the most authoritative and popular Chinese language dictionaries, a project jointly undertaken by the Commercial Press and Oxford U press.

INTRODUCTION

TALKING IN FORKED TONGUES:
Envoicing an Afro-Asiatic Literary Volume

Translation studies continue to gain ground in academic circles especially in the fields of Linguistics, and Literary Studies. This is true of African and Asian academies as it is with the knowledge communities of the rest of the world. The focus on this matter has been almost always with questions of power and language in the vortex of decolonization schools of thought. (See Batchelor, 2014). Indeed, the prominent Kenyan writer and champion of postcolonial languages and their inalienable rights, Ngugi wa Thiong'o, continues to remind us the importance of creating dialogues between languages of the Global South (See Ngugi, 2015, 1986). His works have been translated into tens of languages further underlining the importance of translation studies especially within the larger frame of postcolonial studies. A recent project by young Kenyan writers translated his recent-most short story entitled, "The Upright Revolution: Or Why Humans Walk Upright", into over fifty diverse languages from across Africa in their *Jalada Africa: Translation Issue Volume 1*(2016). The story was first written in Gikuyu under the title, "Ituĩka Rĩa Mũrũngarũ: Kana Kĩrĩa Gĩtũmaga Andũ Mathiĩ Marũngiĩ."

It is clear that the intellectual curiosity around in literature of postcolonial societies cuts across generations and regions. It crosses oceans whether it is the *Kala Pani* or others. It is an important landmark in postcolonial studies indeed. Going against the mainstream translational tendencies of working with European versus African languages only, it breaks and provides a fertile ground for academic inquiry and literary experimentation. Following in such footprints of new thinking in translation approaches to literary rapprochement, our new volume salutes Evan Mwangi's, recent offering, *Translation in African Contexts: Postcolonial Texts, Queer Sexuality and Cosmopolitan Fluency* (2017). Mwangi highlights the nature and notion of translation as an epistemological framework of handling thematics of literatures from the Global South even further.

The exciting Kenyan experiences and epistemic impulses of Ngugi, *Jalada* Africa and Mwangi are not unique. However, they capture transnational and interdisciplinary anxieties of inter-regional cultural awakenings and awarenesses with synechdochical clarity. One that merges intercultural discourses and transcultural expressions forged towards a common humanistic agenda and in support of other cogent reflections on global literary translations in Africa and beyond (See:Bandia, 2015; Adejunmobi, 2014; Batchelor, 2014; Inggs and Meintjes, 2009 among others). It is out of this broadening of horizons of aesthetic, philological and cosmopolitan thought that we evolved this inter-continental project.

This new volume on Translation and Literatures at the nexus of unfolding interlocutions between Africa and Asia has been mooted in the philological spirit of glocalisation captured above. The incipital scholarly essay in *Writing Language, Culture and Development, Africa Vs Asia, Volume 1*, by Lemuel Odeh, we are taught there is strong and validated evidence that Asia and Africa have had close relationships for centuries since the classical period. Of course it is a well-documented fact that modern man originated in Africa with Asia being a focal dispersal point to the rest of the world. Close sharing of ideas and culture between people of these regions exists since time immemorial. This can be deciphered and umbricated from the family stories of Audrey McCombs, Ayo Oyeku and Mona Lisa Jena, that delve into traditional African and Asian family settings and their breakdown with encroachment from various facets, forces and fulcra of unfolding modernities. The syncretic and synchronic cross-fertilization of discourses, discomforts and dynamics at the nexus of the locutions and interlocutions between the two continents is well documented and known. From ancient Religion to mercantilian subjugation, from modern slavery to merchant sojourns, from adventure-instigated flights of reality or fantasy to culinary delights, texts both oral and written abound that highlight the umbilical tie between the two regions. Verses with anchorage in this complex epistemic and gnoseological vista are exemplified by the ancestral modes of aesthetics captured by the sublime art of Smeetha Bhoumik, Vinita Agrawal, and Nureni Ibrahim. Coins own two sides.

The contra-perspective on the otherwise symbiotic nexus between the two regions is saliently raised by the vices transacted across the Indian Ocean, which, like a hip joint, merges Asia and Africa. Take the case of Rhino poaching addressed by Jill Hedgecock in this collection. Her work explores the devastating poaching of the African rhino, which is fueled by the illegal Asian trade of rare horns and their usage in traditional medicine theatres. It is these interrelationships among many complex others in this book that vindicates this anthology as an open arena of discourse and thought.

Note-worthy is that this new anthology is a continuing series of cross-continental, literary anthologies, with the first one already out in print as, *Experimental Wring, African Vs Latin America, Volume 1* (2017). Several others are under preparation. Collectively, these anthologies, hopefully, will instigate renewed anti-hermetic energies across the World academia to share ideas across continents in a dialogic mode of cogitation inspired by inter- and trans- disciplinary paradigms of Gnosis that transcend the postcolonial. Ours is a focused agenda that deliberately offers platforms for artistic and philosophical confrontation of the latent and salient limits of our globalized arena and era through the spoken and written word of aesthetic worth.

Writing Language, Culture and Development focuses on issues to do with practical translation and its action on contemporary literary texts of Asia and Africa as well as the dialogic and aesthetic possibilities between them. From this standpoint we engaged major languages of the region both creatively and critically under the auspices of Translation Studies, a fast growing humanistic field in the Global South. In this volume one finds artistic and philosophical work in Chinese, Japanese, Nepalese, Arabic, Russian, Korean, Kiswahili, Shona, Hausa, Idoma, Igbo, Akan Twi, and of course, English, the global lingua franca of our time. In this respect, this tome is a globophone celebration of languages as intangible assets of our shared human heritage. As noted already the other aspect about this anthology is culture, and as we noted in the call for work, this is another area where these congenital regions have excelled and exported such excellences to the rest of the world. Here is the edited call we sent out as an invitation to submissions to this exciting anthology.

WRITING ON LANGUAGE, CULTURE AND DEVELOPMENT: AFRICA Vs ASIA (VOLUME 1)

Africa and Asia contain over 77% of the world's population and over60 percent of the world's languages and cultures. The two epic continents have lately witnessed leaps in development despite endemic, systemic and epidemic problems of multidimensional manifestation. As we march into the21ˢᵗ century and beyond, thetwo continents will most probably shape the direction the world would take as can already be seen with the mutative influence that Asia has on the world's economy now and especially on Africa and it's facets of existential and practical thought. So we believe these three aspects, namely, language, culture and development form a formidable forum for fostering interaction and interlocution between the continents under the South-South paradigm of recent globalization thought.

Subsequently, we are looking for imaginative writing that addresses or raises these issuescompetently using any genre of literary expression. Send us your best literary fictions, non-fictions, plays, poetry, mixed genres etc... in these languages: *English, languages of the Indian Subcontinent (Hindi, Bengali, Assamese, Malayalam etc.), Kiswahili, Japanese, Korean, Thai and Chinese. Submissions in any other languages from these two continents other than the ones named are welcome. English being the global lingua franca, we welcome translations in this language together with texts submitted in languages of Africa and Asia. Send work in only one genre of your choice. Poetry (3 poems per poet, preferably short poems but we are still open for long poems)Prose, plays and mixed genres (One piece per writer, of not more than 5000 words)*

We are going to have every entry we select translated into another language among those languages we are focusing on, i.e., English, Chinese, Kiswahili and Indian languages, but we are also open to any writing in any indigenous language from these two continents, but these as we have noted, must be accompanied with a translation into English. We will decide after selection and translations whether we will publish a single multi-languages volume or several volumes.

Work must be sent in only one attached document, also include your contact details in this document, i.e., Postal address, Tel no, Email address and a bio note of not more than 100 words.

This project will be edited and translated by the following writers and thinkers:
Tendai R Mwanaka
Wanjohi wa Makokha
Upal Deb

Please send and copy your entries to all the editors:
Tendai R. Mwanaka at mwanaka13@gmail.com, Wanjohi wa Makokha at makokha.justus@ku.ac.ke , Upal Deb at upal.deb@gmail.com,

Closing date for entries is 30 April 2017

NB: Please adhere to the submission guidelines and exercise strict intellectual and artistic integrity.

Indeed, we received a lot of entries from the two conntinents and their polyglossic denizens. We are thankful to all those who submitted to our call, and grateful to those we selected. In terms of content and composition, this volume, *Writing Language, Culture and Development* has 2 essays, 6 stories, 63 poems, 2 plays, and 50 translations into 13 languages from affected critics and multicultural poets who reside, *inter alia,* in: South Africa, Japan, Vietnam, Nepal, China, Korea, Rusia, Tunisia, Nigeria, India, USA, Canada, Australia, Italy, Zimbabwe, Ghana, Kenya, and the UK, who are connected to these two continents, Asia and Africa.

Nurturing South-South interactions and interlocutions, spiritually is an open ended discourse and praxis. We envision this groundbreaking idea as testament to future cooperations between the two continents. We believe Africa and Asia can use their competencies, i.e., human capital, culture, and langauges, histories, and deconstructionist agendas, to create developmental competences and this book highlights and explore a number of pathways that creatives of the two lands can explore and exploit as they march into a future of *Weltliteratur.* The cast and nature of the book and its content is a product of thought, imagination and environment. We invite you to it's offerings that individually, and collectively, accentuate our allied artistic commitment to the Humanities as an arena of thought on identities, languages, cultures, histories and epistemologies of postcolonial posture. Aluta continua.

Tendai Rinos Mwanaka
Wanjohi wa Makokha
Upal Deb
2018

References

Adejunmobi, Moradewun. "Translation and Postcolonial Identity: African Writing and European Languages." *The Translator.* 2014. Pp. 163-81.

Bandia, Paul F., "Introduction: Orality and Translation." *Translation Studies.* 2015. Pp. 125-27.

Batchelor, Kathryn. "Postcolonial Issues in Translation: The African Context." In Sanda Bermann and Catherine Porter, Eds. *A Companion to Translation Studies.* Wiley-Blackwell: New York, 2014. Pp. 246-58.

Inggs, Judith & Libby Meintjes. (Eds.) *Translation Studies in Africa.* New York: Continuum, 2009.

Mwangi, Evan Maina. *Translation in African Contexts: Postcolonial Texts, Queer Sexuality, and Cosmopolitan Fluency.* Kent: Kent State University Press, 2017.

Wa Thiong'o, Ngugi. *Decolonising the Mind: Politics of Language in African Literature.* London: James Currey, 1986.

_____. *In The House of the Translator: A Memoir.* New York: Anchor, 2015.

_____. "The Upright Revolution or Why Humans Walk Upright.". in *Jalada Africa: Translation Issue Volume 1*. Nairobi: Jalada Africa. 2016.

Non fiction

INTRODUCTION TO INTERNATIONAL STUDIES (RELATIONS) IN WEST AFRICA UP TO 1500: CHINESE, EUROPEAN AND ARAB CONNECTIONS

By Lemuel Ekedegwa Odeh Ph.D. (Nigeria)

Abstract

History records revolutionary stages in arts, philosophy, medicine, engineering and sciences that have impacted on man and his environment, including diplomatic ties. All knowledge are historical. International Studies logically has been built on achievements of those relations in the past. Trans-Saharan trade was not merely an economic phenomenon, it connected West Africa to the Mediterranean world on intellectual and diplomatic level. Sino-African relations are traced to pre-modern period. Accordingly historical records, contacts between Africans and Chinese began in the second century B.C., continued on friendly terms from Tang through Song, and Ming Dynasties and interrupted only in the 15th century by the advent of European colonialism. The period of transatlantic slave trade, up to the period of colonisation and Neo-colonialism, shows the effects and consequences of economic relationship between Africa and Europeans. When the Portuguese first sailed down the Atlantic coast of Africa in 1430's, they were interested in one thing. Surprisingly, given modern perspectives, it was not slaves but gold. This was fuelled by the famous magnificent pilgrimage of Mansa Musa in 1324, the visit was remembered in Cairo for centuries afterwards. It was certainly witnessed by Italian traders. The picture of King Musse Melly appeared in European maps for his spending during his pilgrimage. Another equally sensational event was the pilgrimage of Askia Muhammad of Songhay. This paper therefore traces the historical and analytical voyage of this intercourse using a multidisciplinary approach arriving at the various events that brought international studies in the West Africa.

Key words: International studies, Diplomatic level, Trans-Saharan trade, Sino-Africa relations and Pilgrimage

Introduction

The study of international studies (IS) has always been subsumed within the study of History since time in memorial (up to 1500), until very recently, just like Political Science, it became a separate discipline. Nevertheless, history has remained the foundation of a meaningful study of this important subject whose beginning was also historically determined. Although, serious study of international studies began after the First World War, (Thurstan S, 1976) issues and circumstances bordering on International Studies has been with man since its existence.

The frequent conflicts, wars and wholesome destruction of properties had always led man to serious soul searching as to how to prevent future conflicts, how to live in peace and harmony with fellow man since man started cohabiting with fellow man, which is the basis for the International Studies. But the study took a dramatic turn in the 19th century when the study started emphasizing on the development of the international history from the end of the Second World War in 1945 until the end of the Cold War in 1989, with special attention to the foreign policies of the Soviet Union and the United States. The study also deal with topics such as domestic and external factors shaping foreign policy; the origins and course of the Cold War including détente and the end of the Cold War; East-West relations in Europe; European integration; the external relations of Asia and the Middle East, particularly with the Soviet Union and the United States; the Soviet Union's relations with eastern Europe; decolonization and conflict in the developing world. (Thurstan S., 1976)

Diplomatic Relations between Africa and the World Before 1500

The academic discipline of history had provided a serious scholarship and the broadest knowledge of International Studies available to man. History had been able to keep all the records of the revolutionary advances in the arts, philosophy, medicine, engineering and sciences that have left their impact on man and his environment, including the diplomatic ties that had existed. That is why it is said that all knowledge is historical. International Studies logically had been built on the achievements of those relations which had been toiled in the same field in the past.

Origins of the Trans-Saharan Contacts

In spite of her vast geographical dimensions and natural extremes, the Sahara was never a barrier which had completely isolated Black Africa from other civilizations, in the same sense as the Atlantic Ocean separated the New World from the Old. The regular commercial and cultural exchange between Africa and the Mediterranean world did not start properly until the 8th century AD. Yet the beginning of trans-Saharan trade was not such a sudden and dramatic event like the coming of Europeans to America, but it had a long history of sporadic encounters for more than 1000 years. When and how the very first contacts took place is still obscure, although their origins can be traced already to the prehistoric times. (Alistair B., 1962)

The establishment and success of regular trans-Saharan trade which brought about the diplomatic relation to Africa as at that period, for example, was not possible without the active participation of Africans who understood perfectly well, how to utilize the new opportunities offered by the commercial contacts to the Islamic world. The Garamantes (or alternatively some other Saharan people) had carried West African gold and Ivory to the markets of Carthage and to the desert edge, Sahil, or "the shore"(Alistair B., 1962) for barter with the goods that came outside of Africa, and to established diplomatic deals with the Arabs who promised them protections and weapons in return. The trans-Saharan trade was not merely an economic phenomenon, but it connected Western Africa to the Mediterranean world on the intellectual and diplomatic level, too. Listening to the tales of traders, the medieval Arab geographers learnt to know the sub-Saharan Africa which they called Bilad al-Sudan, "The Land of the Blacks", although their knowledge covered only the areas lying close to the desert edge, Sahil, or "the shore". (Elise H. n.d)

The real initiators of trans-Saharan trade were the Berber nomads who frequently crossed the desert with their camel flocks. ((Elise H. n.d) The nomads, who resided at southern edge of Sahara, left to the north in the beginning of the rainy season, returning back by the eve of the dry season. While staying in their pastures in southern Morocco and the Atlas mountains, these nomads have certainly met people who, in their turn, had contacts beyond the Roman limes. As the nomads learned to know the great value of gold in Roman world, they perhaps started bartering it from the peoples of West Africa for salt and copper. The gold was carried to the north, where it was probably used for payment of dates, corn and such handicrafts which the nomads could not produce themselves. The nomads may have bought also some luxury objects made in the Roman world, which they bartered for gold in the south. This trade could have started only after the adoption of dromedary by the Saharan peoples, for horses do not survive in the harsh conditions of the desert. The camels were important not so much as mounts than beasts of burden, for they enabled transportation efficiently both the merchandises and the food and water which were needed during the crossing of the desert (Michael C, 1978); the traders usually walked all the way.

According to the survived classical sources, ancient geographers believed that after the fertile North African littoral began nothing but a vast, arid, hot and uninhabited desert. (Michael C, 1978). The same can be said of West Africans who were presumably not aware of the existence of Mediterranean peoples either. Secondly, the volume of the trade must have been humble, for the Roman Empire made no effective efforts to expand her political dominance beyond the limes. Neither had the Romans any economic reason to develop closer commercial and diplomatic relations with the unknown lands in the south, because they obtained all the merchandise the Africans could offer them, namely gold, ivory, exotic beasts and slaves, more easily within her own borders or from the nearby frontier areas in Europe and the Middle East. Similarly, the Roman world had very few products which could have encouraged the Africans to increase the volume of trade. But this could not be said of the later centuries to come.

China and Africa Relations

Sino-African relations can be traced back to pre-modern period. According to historical records, contacts between Africans and Chinese began in the second century B.C. and continued on friendly terms from Tang through Song, and Ming Dynasties and were interrupted only in the 15th century by the advent of European colonialism. (Li Z., 2002)   In the initial stage of the Sino-African relations, Minghui posits that Egyptian Queen Cleopatra dresses were made of silk acquired from China. (Kong M., 2003). Later in the 15th century, Zheng He, the legendary Chinese navigator undertook seven voyages along the east coast of Africa landing at places known today as Kenya, Madagascar, and Somalia. Zheng He took Chinaware, silk, and tea to east coast of Africa. The east Africans reciprocated with among other treasures, giraffes and zebras which Zheng He took back to China. These animals are "regarded as auspicious animals symbolic of good fortune and happiness" in Chinese culture. (Li Z. 2002). The 15th century is generally regarded as an important era in Sino-African relations because, not only were goods and envoys exchanged, but so were scientific and technological exchanges. (Farah A., n.d.) During that period, Africans and Chinese also exchanged envoys and maintained friendly ties based on mutual respect characterized by the generally speaking, peace loving culture of the two groups. As such, there have not been any recorded historical accounts of wars of pacification between the Chinese and Africans. Neither have there been claims of the Chinese raiding rural areas to plunder, enslave, occupy, and colonize Africans. (David S. &Joshua E., 2012). Ironically, it was Western colonialism and imperialism of both groups that terminated the peaceful relationship that existed between Africans and the Chinese in the pre-colonial era. In a way, Sino-African relations were defined in a significant way by external factors. First, it was Western colonialism: then after that it was the Cold War that took place just before the Cultural Revolution.

Africa and Europe Relations

There is no way one can make an attempt to holistically appraise the relations between the people of Africa and Europeans, without giving a brief history of the economic contacts between the people of African regions and people from outside the region starting from the period before the contact with the Arabs about 400B.C to about 700AD, to the period of transatlantic slave trade, up to the period of colonization and Neo-colonialism. It specifically shows the effects and consequences of the economic relationship between Africa and the Europeans.

The relations have been in stages. We have the period before the impact of the Islamic world that is about 400.BC to 700 A.D. (Basil D., 1964) Throughout this period, there will have been many parts of Africa which had no contacts with the outside, and in most cases such contacts as there were with the classical world were slender, sporadic and indirect. The connection between Europe and North Africa is older than recorded history. It seems clear that cultural influences crossed the Mediterranean barrier during the late Paleolithic and Neolithic ages. Hence, the late Paleolithic Aterian industry and Caspian culture, both from the North Africa, are connected with Europe. Some early Neolithic influence may have arrived in Europe from North Africa.

But Europe was never in a hurry to establish direct diplomatic relation with the people of the sub-Saharan Africa probably because the European ancient geographers believed that after the fertile North African littoral began nothing but a vast, arid, hot and uninhabited desert existed. The same can be said of West Africans who were presumably not aware of the existence of European peoples either. Secondly, the volume of the trade must have been humble, for the Europeans made no effective efforts to expand her political dominance beyond the limes. Neither had they any economic reason to develop closer commercial contacts with the unknown lands in the south, because they obtained all the merchandize the West Africans could offer them, namely gold, ivory, exotic beasts and slaves, more easily within her own borders or from the nearby frontier areas in Europe and the Middle East. Similarly, the Roman world had very few products which could have encouraged the West Africans to increase the volume of trade.

However, the entire situation changed as the demand for the goods of the West African people began to increase in not only Europe, but other parts of the world. Some of the factors that alerted the Europeans to develop direct contact and diplomatic relations with the people of Africa can be summarized under socio-economic factors as discussed below:

Pilgrimage

When the first West African Muslims started to visit Mecca for Pilgrimage (Pilgrimage to Mecca is one of the five pillars of Islam, and in principle an obligation for all Muslims) (Basil D., 1964), they were mainly nobles and rulers who had the economic possibilities to perform the long journey. Especially the rulers of Mali became famous for their sumptuous pilgrimages, the first of which is said to have taken place in the 1260s. Yet the most famous was the

35

magnificent pilgrimage of Mansa Musa in 1324, whose visit was remembered in Cairo for centuries afterwards. It was certainly witnessed by Italian traders, too. The picture of King Musse Melly appeared in European maps for his spending during his pilgrimage. Another equally sensational event was the pilgrimage of Askia Muhammad of Songhay. (Adebayo O., 1997) The most popular route to Mecca went through Cairo, which was the greatest and most important city in the eastern Mediterranean. However, some of the pilgrims presumably visited also other cities in the Middle East. At least, European explorers met many African pilgrims who had visited not only Cairo and Mecca but also Jerusalem, Baghdad, Damascus and even Istanbul. In these large cosmopolitan cities, the Africans were able to meet people from many other countries, including Europeans who later stuck diplomatic deals and obtained the right to establish their first permanent trading settlements in some strategic parts of Africa. (Adebayo O., 1997)

Lust for Gold

When the Portuguese first sailed down the Atlantic coast of Africa in the 1430's, they were interested in one thing. Surprisingly, given modern perspectives, it was not slaves but gold. Ever since Mansa Musa, the king of Mali, made his pilgrimage to Mecca in 1325, with 500 slaves and 100 camels (each carrying gold) the region had become synonymous with such wealth. (Herodotus, Transi. Aubrey S., 1954). There was one major problem: trade from sub-Saharan Africa was controlled by the Islamic Empire which stretched along Africa's northern coast. Muslim trade routes across the Sahara, which had existed for centuries, involved salt, kola, textiles, fish, grain, and slaves. As the Portuguese extended their influence and established diplomatic ties around the west coast, Mauritania, Senegambia (by 1445) and Guinea, they created trading posts. Rather than becoming direct competitors to the Muslim merchants, the expanding market opportunities in Europe and the Mediterranean resulted in increased trade across the Sahara. (Historia Universal Sigio XXI, 1972)

In addition, the Portuguese merchants gained access to the interior via the Senegal and Gambia rivers which bisected long-standing trans-Saharan routes. At the beginning of the trade, The Portuguese brought in copper ware, cloth, tools, wine and horses. (Trade goods soon included arms and ammunition.) In exchange, the Portuguese received gold (transported from mines of the Akan deposits), pepper (a trade which lasted until Vasco da Gama reached India in 1498) and ivory. (AdemolaO. 2008)

By-Passing the Muslims Monopoly

With the expansion of Islam in the middle Ages, North Africa was culturally cut off from non-Muslim Europe. The Islamic Empire created barrier between Europe and the rest of the world, with European traders paying heavy tributes to obtain prized commodities like West Africa gold, East Asian spices and silk among others. In addition, the Jews of modern Spain, Portugal and Morocco were allowed in both cultural regions. Among them were Abraham Cresques and his son Jehuda, whose 1375 Catalan Atlas improved European knowledge of Africa and other regions, with a good deal of Muslim geographical knowledge and some educated guesses and imagination to fill in the blanks. This Atlas detailed the Catalan expedition of Jaume Ferrer to Gold River in 1346, which according to the map went south of Cape Bojador and to what is called West Africa Finisterrae. (Ademola O., 2008)

The Europeans found Muslim merchants monopoly entrenched along the African coast as far as the Bight of Benin. The Slave Coast, as the Bight of Benin was known, was reached by the Portuguese at the start of the 1470's. It was not until they reached the Kongo coast in the 1480's that they outdistanced Muslim trading territory and obtained permission (diplomatic relation) to establish their forts and trading posts. The first of the major European trading 'forts', Elmina, was founded on the Gold Coast in 1482. (Vincent B. K. 1994). Elmina (originally known as Sao Jorge de Mina) was modeled on the Castello de Sao Jorge, the first of the Portuguese Royal residence in Lisbon. Elmina, which of course, means the mine, became a major trading center for slaves purchased along the Slave Rivers of Benin.

The Genoese were also interested in circumventing the Muslim monopoly on Asian trade. In 1291, Tedisio Doria ordered Vandino and Ugolino Vivaldi to reach India via the Atlantic Ocean, which brought about the reaching of West Africa through the Atlantic coast. (Guisep R.A., n.d.). By the beginning of the colonial era there were forty such forts operating along the coast. Rather than being icons of colonial domination, the forts acted as trading posts - they rarely saw military action - the fortifications were important, however, when arms and ammunition were being stored prior to trade.

Africa and the Arabs

The earliest time that Africa and the Arab established relation also known in history as the Islamic contact period was about A.D 700-AD 1475. For the first time we moved into a period of African history when long distance trade, however indirect, begin to play an increasingly important role in powerfully influencing not only economic but social and political patterns as well of the Arab-African relations. (Hopkins A. G., 1964). The relation mostly in terms of trade brought wealth to certain parts of Africa, and this helped to provide the basis for social stratification and state formation. People mined rock salt in the Sahara and evaporated sea salt along the coast. Other regions concentrated on cotton, and textile. As a result regular patterns of trade helped to exchange the surplus from one region with others. The trade encouraged the growth of small towns, some near the desert-edge to profit from Trans-Saharan trade like Timbouktou, Agadez, Ciao and Onalata.

The conditions of trans-Saharan trade changed remarkably after Northern Africa became a part of the Islamic world in the late 7th century AD. The vast Umayyid caliphate, reaching from the slopes of Pyrenees to the banks of Indus, formed a solid market area for which Islam was the forced religion and the monetary system of which was based on gold. In practice, it meant that this precious metal had a great demand throughout the Islamic world. In the eastern parts of the caliphate, gold could be obtained sufficiently from local mines or by recycling the ancient hoards. In the western parts, the situation was more difficult, for there are no gold mines in Northern Africa. (Hopkins A. G., 1964). However, the Muslim rulers in the west struck their own golden dinars. Since there is no evidence that they had imported gold from Egypt or the Middle East, they must have obtained it from other sources. Plausible alternatives are the mines of Sicily and southern Spain, which were known already in ancient times, and the existing Roman and Byzantine treasures. Yet part of the metal was inevitably brought from Western Africa. In fact, it seems that regular and intensive trade across the desert was organised quite soon after the Arabs had consolidated their power in Northern Africa: both the major northern terminals of the trans-Saharan routes, Sijilmasa and Tahert, were founded in mid-8th century AD. However, the trade could succeed only because it managed to join up with the internal West African commercial network. By the arrival of first North African traders, perhaps in the early 8th century, the peoples of the savanna had already established large states, like Ghana and Gao, and cities, like Jenne which had some twenty thousand inhabitants which then the Arabs struggled to establish diplomatic ties with so as to enable them to continue to carry out various transactions. But new cities were also born at the desert edge, like Awdaghust, Kumbi Saleh and Tadamakka, and their destiny was tied closely with the continuity of the long distance trade: when the caravan routes later changed and the volume of trade declined, these towns, too, were soon abandoned. There were three basic routes across the Sahara: the "western", leading from Sijilmasa to Awdaghust; the "central", and the most important, leading from

Ifriqiya to the Niger bend; and the "northern" otherwise known as the Egyptian trade route, leading from Egypt to the Niger bend via Siwa and Kufra, which was, however, abandoned in the 10th century as it was too dangerous. (PekkaM. n.d.) Very little is known about the volume of the trans-Saharan trade during the first Islamic centuries. According to the contemporary Arabic sources, the caravans brought to the north annually huge amounts of gold, but modern estimates range from 2,000 to 3,000 kg per year[13]. Nevertheless, a real boom in the trade began in the 10th century, with the establishment of the Fatimid caliphate in Northern Africa in 910. The reason was that the Fatimids, who were in rivalry both with the Umayyads of Spain and the Abbasids of Baghdad, needed constantly lots of gold to finance their continuous wars and extensive religious propaganda. That made them to continue to look for allies and establishing diplomatic ties with the Arabs. The rise of Fatimids also meant that the western route became the most important, since their access to the central route was blocked by the Ibadites who still held Wargla. Yet the transfer of the Fatimid capital from Ifriqiya to Egypt in 971 caused a brief period of stagnation in the trade. Residing in Cairo, the Fatimid caliphs were no more interested in North African affairs, since they could obtain gold more easily from Nubian mines. A second boom took place in the late 11th century, as the Almoravids united Western Sahara, Morocco and Islamic Spain into a single empire. Like the Fatimids, the Almoravids needed also a lot of gold to finance their wars against the Christians in Spain and the rebelling Almohads in Maghreb. During the Almoravid period, gold seems to have flowed to the north with great amounts, for the Almoravid golden dinars became the most common and esteemed currency in the Mediterranean area, including the Christian world. A brief period of stagnation was followed after the downfall of Almoravids in 1147, but the trade continued steadily again from the mid-13th century until the Moroccan invasion in Timbuktu in 1591. (Walter R. 1973)

The diplomatic relations between the Arabs and African cultures was peaceful, and it can be termed "controlled relationship". This concept is usually applied to the European encounter with China, where foreign traders were forced to obey the rules set by the Chinese government which decided unilaterally on the location of trade, the number of traders, as well as type and character of the goods. If the Europeans were not willing to accept these rules, they were not permitted to continue their trade. (Philip D. C. 1976). Before the outbreak of the First Opium War in 1839, the Chinese empire was powerful enough to reject all military threats from the part of European naval powers.

In Africa, the contact zone was limited to the desert edge cities, where North African traders were isolated for their own quarters, lying usually outside the local dwelling. Yet there was no racial discrimination. In fact, many of the traders took local concubines, as no women of their own society were available. This behaviour is understandable, for the traders had often to spend several years in the south, and there lived also permanent agents of North African trading companies. Afterwards twin cities, with separate quarters for the Muslim and non-Muslim population, became a common structure for urban settlements throughout Western Africa. On the other hand, the isolation of North African traders was partly voluntary for two reasons. First, the West African interior was as unhealthy for Arabs as the coastal area was for Europeans, and thus the traders were not willing to leave the desert edge cities where the conditions were healthier. Secondly, by isolating themselves, the traders were able to maintain their own culture and practice their own religion. Otherwise the traders had to follow local laws and customs, regardless whether they were against the Quranic law. But the cultural difference was recognized, and the traders were not intentionally forced to do such things which they felt offending.

Before the European discovery of America, West African mines were the most important single source of gold both for Northern

Africa and Europe; it is estimated that two-thirds of all the gold circulating in the Mediterranean area in the Middle Ages was imported across the Sahara. (Omo J.U., 1986). This made the uninterrupted continuity of trade more important for North African rulers than their West African counterparts. The North African rulers could not obtain gold for their coins elsewhere.

However, the position of the powerful states of the West African savanna was not based on the possession of the gold reserves, but on the control over the principal trade routes leading from the desert edge terminals to the gold fields in the south. In this way, the rulers of northern savanna could monopolize the trade, and they strictly prevented the Arabs to establish any direct contacts with the actual producers of gold. Inside Western Africa, the diplomatic ties were carried on by local brokers, or the Dyula. The other reason was that the Arab traders were without the protection provided by their own civilization, while staying in sub-Saharan Africa. Before the wider introduction of firearms in the 16th century, the Arab rulers of Northern Africa had no real possibilities to threaten their West African counterparts with war, as there were no such differences between the military technologies which guaranteed them any absolute superiority. Besides the desert, another natural advantage which protected the West Africans was the unhealthy environment. Most parts of the savanna are infected by trypanosomiasis, which is lethal especially for quadrupeds, thus preventing the large scale use of cavalry forces in this area.

The last stage of the relation before 1500 was known as the coastal contact period about A.D 1475-1850, this marked the period that the relation was marred with both the trans-Saharan and trans-Atlantic slave trade that devastated the African region which many scholars had continue to argue was responsible for the underdevelopment of the African continent. However, during this period their activities were mainly along the coast. There are no records concerning the volume of trans-Saharan slave trade, but it is estimated that during the long period which lasted for about thousands of years, which followed its beginning in the 8th century AD, about 9.3 million black slaves were imported to the north, including those who died during the painful crossing of the desert. (Young J.W. &Kent J., 2003). In fact, the total quantity of trans-Saharan slave trade was a little less equal to the Atlantic trade, though its annual volume was much lower. However, no great black communities were born in Northern Africa in the same sense as those in the American colonies, for most of the slaves were women whose fertility in slavery was low. The offspring of black concubines with their Arab masters were free and merged gradually into the North African population, although is some areas they were also killed. Therefore, mortality of slaves had to be replaced by importing new ones, and the overall amount of black slaves who were actually present in Northern Africa remained thus restrained.

Notes and References

A. G Hopkins, *"The Economic History of West Africa"* 1964, London, Longman, p. 12

Adebayo Olukoshi, *'West Africa Political Economy in The Next Millennium',* 1997, *www.lodesra-org/ma/pds/Adebayo-Olukoshi.p.d.f,* Retrieved on 18/12/12

AdemolaOgunlowa, *'Before the Beginning' Article in Tell magazine February 18, 2008 page 16-26*

Alistair Boddy, *'Origin of the Trans-Saharan Slave Trade'.* 1962, London, Evans, p. 15

Basil Davidson, *The African Past',* 1964, Penguin, Harmondsworth, p.5

D. C Philip, *"The Atlantic Slave Trade 1600-1800" In Ajayi Crowther (ed) History of West Africa 1976, vol. 1 Longman Limited*

David Shinn and Joshua Eisenmann. *China and Africa: A Century of Engagement, chapter 2. 2012.*

Elise Hullery, 'The Impact of European Settlement within French West Africa'. *In Did Pre Colonial Prosperous Areas Fall Behind? www.dial.prdfr. Retrieved on 18/12/12*

Farah Arbab, *"China-Africa Interaction: Prospects for a Strategic Partnership." Institute of Strategic Studies.*

Herodotus, Transl. *Aubrey de Selincourt, Penguin, Harmondsworth, 1954*

Historia Universal Sigio XXI. *Africa: desde la prehitoria hasta los anossesenta. Pierre Bertaux, 1972. Sigio XXI Editores S.A ISBN 84-323-0069-1 edited*

J. Hanhimaki and O.A. Westad, *The Cold War. A History in Documents and Eyewitness Accounts (Oxford: Oxford University Press, 2003)*

J.U. Omo, 'Economics, *An African Perspective' 1986, London, John West Publications Limited, p. 6*

J.W. Young and J. Kent, *International Relations since 1945: A Global History (Oxford: Oxford University Press, 2003)*

Kong Minghui, *"Sino-African Relations and China's Policy towards Africa." Bureau of International Cooperation. Chinese Academy of Social Sciences, 2003.*

Li Zhao Xing, *"Forging a New Chapter in Sino-African Friendship and Cooperation" in China Facts and Figures 2002.*

Michael Crowder, *'The Story of West Africa People'*, 1978, London, Evans, p.6-7

Pekka Masonen *"The European Exploration of Africa"*. The Author and Nordic Society for Middle Eastern Studies. Archived 18.8.95

R.A Guisep, *'Africa and the Africans In the Age Of The Atlantic Slave Trade'*. A project by History World International. Vol. 1, No.1 p.11

Thurstan Shaw. *'The Pre History of West Africa'* in Ajayi Crowther (ed) History of West Africa, 1976, Vol.1, Longman Limited, p. 23

Vincent B. Khapoya, *'The African Experience'*, 1994, Prentice Hall, Upper Saddle River, New Jersey, p.32

Walter Rodney. *'How Europe Underdeveloped Africa'* Bolgle-L'overture Publication, London, 1973

RHINO-CIDE
By Jill Hedgecock

What I know of rhinos started in Africa. What I know of rhino poaching spans both the African and Asian continents. While 80 percent of these horned animals live in South Africa, their population declines are largely being driven by the Asian black market. While human encroachment into their territories in Africa are also a concern from the expansion of cattle ranching, the death rate of the African rhinos has reached staggering numbers in recent years in large part due to the skyrocketing price for their horns in Asia. According to the *World Wildlife Fund*, about 96 percent of African black rhinos were lost to large-scale poaching between 1970 and 1992 and the losses keep rising. If the rhino is to be saved, major changes will need to happen across both countries, including a cultural shift in Asia away from the view that rhino horn contains curative properties.

Five rhino species remain on this planet: three reside in Asia and two in Africa. All rhinos carry many of the same features, including a tiny almond-shaped eye nestled amidst the bags and wrinkles of flesh and Calla-lily shaped ears, but they are each uniquely suited to provide an important role in the environment—a function that has potential widespread repercussions if lost. In the early 19th century, the rhino population was estimated to be one million. In 1970, their numbers fell to around 70,000 or seven percent of their peak population. In 2016, around 28,000 rhinos are reported to remain in the wild. Three of the five remaining rhino species have declined so severely that they have been designated as critically endangered. And all share one troubling trait: they are being killed for profit.

And it isn't only these monolithic gray creatures that are at risk. The loss of rhinos could affect the survival of other species not to mention negative impacts to local economies, which can further increase human suffering in already destitute situations. In addition to being a draw for tourists, rhinos have been used symbolically by tribal leaders to gain respect and used for cultural traditions such as rainmaking rituals. [i] These giant herbivores also serve a critical function in maintaining a healthy ecosystem. [ii] A 5,000-pound white rhino can consume fifty or more pounds of food in one day. But it isn't only the sheer bulk of vegetation consumed that makes them so important. Unlike elephants that browse on trees, rhinos act as giant weed whackers, selectively grazing on certain plants and grasses, creating biodiversity in the landscape. These dietary preferences also create a mosaic patchwork of habitat that is more attractive for other grazers such as zebra and antelope, who, in turn, are food for lions, leopards, and hyenas. Thus, extinction of rhinos can impact the survival of many more species as well adversely impact long-standing native cultural traditions and tribal livelihood.

The poaching problem will not be easy to solve. Asian criminal syndicates, corrupt African game wardens, and criminal transportation officials—they all speak the universal language of money and are to blame for the rapid escalation in African rhino deaths. Fueled by demand from Chinese and Southeastern Asian consumers whose culture promotes the erroneous belief that the keratinous material of rhino horn provides medicinal cures for a range of illnesses from hangovers to cancer, well-organized criminal organizations have capitalized on the misinformation.

The demand for the keratinous material that makes up the rhino horn continues to grow in the Asian culture. Rhino horn has been traditionally used to treat fevers, but fake news is promoting the misguided belief that horn powder cures everything from hangovers to impotence to cancer has created a frenetic seller's market, driven largely by China. [iii] Top dollar is spent on purchasing essentially the same material as finger nails. In 2014, the Vietnamese Ministry of Health confirmed that rhino horn had no medicinal value, but this has had little impact on demand. The hope is that a Vietnamese education campaign starring celebrities in advertisements will have better success. [iv] If the demand is reduced and the culture shifts toward a more sympathetic view of rhinos, then perhaps more people will develop contempt for poaching.

International attention appears to be raising awareness. England's Prince William, who serves as president of *United for Wildlife*, a consortium of wildlife charities, is a strong advocate for the rhino. In March 2016, he unveiled a global agreement to crack down on wildlife trafficking routes. [v] Forty transportation authorities, representing airline, shipping and custom agency leaders, signed the declaration to stop the transfer of poached animal products into the black market.

Many scientific solutions have been proposed to address the poaching problem. Dehorning, once touted as an ideal solution, has largely failed. Most poachers will still shoot the dehorned animal either to harvest the stub of remaining horn or to avoid tracking a rhino without a horn in the future. According to the *Save the Rhino* website, in the early 1990s in Zimbabwe, the majority of dehorned rhinos were killed by poachers within a year and a half after being dehorned. The dehorning operation is also risky because the animal may die while under anesthesia. Yet, dehorning may still have merit and may not be as harmful as once thought. While it has been suggested that rhinos need their horns to protect themselves and their young, a study of dehorned black rhinos found no significant difference in survival in the young of dehorned black rhino when compared to the offspring of horned rhinos. [vi]

Other options to combat rhino extinction from poaching include poisoning the rhino horn, development of synthetic horn material, legalization of trade, captive breeding farms for sustainable harvesting, improvement of anti-poaching techniques, and relocation of rhinos out of high poaching areas.

Poisoning the horn seemed like a fail-proof solution that would make rhino horns worthless. A colored toxic dye that didn't hurt the rhino was injected into the horn and the outer skin of the rhino's horn was painted a bright color. But poachers soon discovered that the poison didn't penetrate far inside the dense fiber.[vii]

The *International Rhino Foundation* (IRF) opposes the sale of synthetic horns. Critics believe that creating a fake version will drive up the cost of and demand for poached rhino horn. The consequences could mean an even bigger market for a natural product seen as more potent and, therefore, more desirable.

Proponents of sustainable harvesting of rhino horns argue that the horn can be removed humanely and painlessly,[viii]although they admit the procedure does involve anesthetizing the animal, which is not without risk.[ix]

Opponents of legalization suggest it will only worsen the problem because corruption is rampant.[9]. Poaching would still be cheaper and faster than farming due to the low reproductive rate of rhinos. With permits, private rhino owners could sell horns illegally obtained from poached rhinos to circumvent the system for their personal enrichment.[x] Legalization may even increase demand by legitimizing its use for consumers who would not buy an illegal substance, but will after it becomes lawful. The *World Wildlife Fund* reports that the connoisseurs of rhino horn are mainly financially successful Asian men over the age of forty who buy entire horns as a symbol of their wealth. Thus, there are potentially millions of customers waiting for the price to drop.

Anti-poaching efforts have largely failed in most areas of Africa, although exceptions have occurred in some countries such as Botswana, which has managed to reduce rhino losses. The areas where rhinos roam are large, often in terrain with limited sight distance. Poachers are typically outfitted with the latest technology in tracking tools by black market dollars whereas anti-poaching units tend to be underfunded. Thus, when game wardens are provisioned with anti-poaching equipment such as cameras, drones, trained dogs, and night-vision binoculars, they have a better chance of preventing rhino poaching.[xi] A game reserve in Limpopo, a province of South

Africa, reported success using military thermal cameras to track the movements of poachers[xii] after donations of equipment provided by the *Rhino Protection Programme.*

The *Rhinos Without Borders* campaign based in South Africa seeks to relocate rhinos away from high poaching areas. This effort comes with a price tag of $45,000 per rhino. Other efforts to establish a breeding rhino population outside Africa involve the relocation of 80 rhinos from Africa to Australia. With up to a sixteen-month gestation, replenishing wild rhino populations will not happen quickly. Still, these transplants may have a better chance of success than if they were sent to zoos.

Rhinos born in captivity rarely produce young. An exception occurred in California at the San Diego Zoo Safari Park. In April 2016, a southern white rhino was born to a captive female after ten years of breeding efforts.[xiii] The success was attributed to a change in the mother's diet. However, other attempts have not achieved the desired result. Artificial insemination has failed to produce young in the critically endangered northern white rhino.[xiv] While the possibility of using sperm from a male northern white rhino to impregnate the more common southern white rhino has been suggested, gauging the estrus cycle of the female is difficult. Thus, it is unlikely that the rhinos currently living in captivity will be able to save the species from extinction. For the Northern white rhino, a scientific breakthrough will be necessary. Only one male and female remain and these three individuals are all too old to reproduce.

While levels of rhino horn poaching have increased by 5,000 percent since 2007, the trend is shifting. Between 2015 and 2016, 121 fewer rhinos were poached in South Africa. But considering that thirteen rhinos were killed in 2007 compared to 1,054 in 2016, game wardens may occasionally win a battle, but it appears they are still losing the war.

Progress is being made. The number of rhinos killed in South Africa dropped from 1,175 in 2015 to 1,054 in 2016. But even these population decreases are not sustainable and both countries need to band together to find solutions to avoid rhino-cide. If they don't, it's possible that all subspecies of African white rhinos in the wild could vanish in the next twenty years, making it the largest land mammal to become extinct since the woolly mammoth.

There is no equivalent word for genocide in the animal kingdom, but that doesn't mean the act of "rhino-cide" will not achieve the same result. There is no other creature like the rhino on the planet. To watch a grazing rhino is equivalent to travelling back in time to witness the resurrection of an ancient dinosaur. But if this creature is to survive, Africa and Asia need to take measures to protect rhinos where they exist, manage them for population growth, and educate the local community on the value of rhino populations and the time to act is now.

Source Material and Further Reading:

[1]Boreyens, J.C. A. M. and van der Ryst. 2014. *The cultural and symbolic significance of the African rhinoceros: A review of the traditional beliefs, perceptions and practices of agropastoralist societies in southern Africa, South African Humanities 26: 21-55. July.*

[1]Nuwer, R., 2014. *Here's What Might Happen to Local Ecosystems If All the Rhinos Disappear, Smithsonian.com, February 27.http://www.smithsonianmag.com/articles/heres-what-might-happen-local-ecosystems-if-all-rhinos-disappear-180949896/#6GP7XCkSlSdzrCsL.99*

[1]Larson, R. 2010. *Rhino horn: All myth, no medicine, National Geographic Society, July. http://voices.nationalgeographic.com/2010/07/07/rhino_horn_and_tradition al_chinese_medicine_facts/*

[1]Aldred, J. 2016. *Richard Branson fronts nail-biting campaign against rhino poaching,* The Guardian, January 13. https://www.theguardian.com/environment/2016/jan/13/richard-branson-fronts-nail-biting-campaign-against-rhino-poaching

[1]Leithead, A. 2016, *Prince William in plan to tackle wildlife trafficking,* BBC News, March 15, http://www.bbc.com/news/uk-35814135.

[1]Du Toit, R. and N. Anderson., 2013. *Dehorning rhinos. Wildlife Ranching* 2013 *Autumn:* 82-85. http://www.rhinoresourcecenter.com/index.php?s=1&act=refs&CODE=ref_detail&id=1366424580

[1]Ferreira, S., Hofmeyr, M., Pienaar, D., and D. Cooper. 2014. *.Chemical horn infusions: a poaching deterrent or an unnecessary deception?Pachyderm 55:54-61.*

[1]Nuwer, R., 2016. *A tipping point for slaughter. Newsweek 167 (20) Dec 2, 2016: 50-53.*

[1]Hart, A. 2016. *Could legalising the trade in rhino horn save the species? The Biologist 63(6):7.*

[1]Swartz, M. 2016. *Will Keeping the Rhino Horn Trade Illegal Kill More Rhinos?* National Geographic. April. http://voices.nationalgeographic.com/2016/04/23/opinion-will-keeping-the-rhino-horn-trade-illegal-kill-more-rhinos/

[1]Starr, M. 2016. *Can tech save the rhino? Cnet Magazine Winter 2016* November 27, 2016: https://www.cnet.com/news/rhinos-endangered-poaching-synthetic-horn-tech/.

[1] Peace Parks Foundation News. 2015. *Night Vision Equipment for Kruger National Park Rangers, July 10.*

[1] Chiusano, S. 2016. *Southern white rhino gives birth to calf at San Diego Zoo, New York Daily News, April 6. M.nydailynews.com.*

[1] Hubbard, A. and T. Perry. 2014. *Only 5 northern white rhinos are left; artificial insemination difficult, LosAngelesTimes.comDecember. http://www.latimes.com/local/lanow/la-me-ln-white-rhino-dies-safari-park-20141214-story.html*

[1] Starzak, K. 2014. *New study: Infusing rhino horns with poison doesn't work, Earthtouchnews Network, May 30.http://www.earthtouchnews.com/environmental-crime/poaching/new-study-infusing-rhino-horns-with-poison-doesnt-work*

Fiction

A DARK ENERGY, Chapter 11, a novel extract
By Tendai Rinos Mwanaka

They arrived at the graveplace at about three, at three- the self dispossessed hour. At three o'clock they visited the lost hour, that hour that undresses self into itself. They were still some voices rising, some people were singing, some people were speaking, trying to shape reality into ideas, trying to transform the world of words and songs into the reality that faced them. He knew that in this quite place songs will always be sung, voices will always be heard.

The leaves on the vibrant fig tree expressed a surest green. On this Fig tree, to the left of the graveyard, the brain-fever bird was doing twelve-ton scales on its own electronic harmonium. Its songs felt like they were meant for this youthful cadaver that they were now circling. They were a line of shrouded faces circling her, no mist of breathe, every face at the grave place was staring askance at her face, in its intense rehearsal of its own doubt. Some were even afraid that her immortalness would reach out and uncoil around them.

The big green meat flies were also making songs of their own with their engine voices as they hissed around this mangled body. Sometimes those meat flies were also circling, haphazardly, this young cadaver. The people rocked themselves and the land rocked them, thus the people rocked the land, and the songs were slower. The blackness in Don's heart was dripping on a soundless keyboard, creating a harmonium he could only feel but never heard. His brain's lymphatic nodes were bubbling to this piano's keys, dripping clenching ivory whips.

The air around the graveyard was dark even if it was still late afternoon of a summer day, beaten too thick and it had the smell and feel of something being pressed through Don's nostrils and throat forcefully. The feelings inside him were haunting the skin of light, clear and real.

As he made his way in the circled queue of those seeing Lillian's face for the last time, circling her casket and, having a last glimpse of her, he was thinking of what he would experience when his eyes see her face again. He knew he had already entered the world of what-ifs, and the in-betweens.

Is she still alive, serving time? And, he was also thinking.

Will I say a special prayer?

He tried to break-free mentally. He told himself he had to face her with absence of doubt. And then he saw her face which he knew was detached from the rest of the body but had been set in such a way as to make it appear whole, as if a string of some sort had been used to connect those discarded parts. He was amazed by how she did it, creating such perfect wholeness within her decapitated body as if she still was a whole umber shell. Her eyes seemed open and her eyes, now dark, fear unaware, backlit with hope for him, surveyed him with years she wanted for herself. He did not want to think that she had raged and raged as they were slicing her head. Raging against the dying of her light!

"What if she could still feel the pain....?" He didn't want to think that he had always been a soldier of misfortune, that every life and every death is really nonnegotiable. He really wanted something. He wanted to have something that he could hold, that he could own to himself.

And yet his mind confronting this actuality met its own match. There was nothing to really grasp there, that there was nothing perhaps beyond hearing and seeing or even the omission of these things. *Is she in the half way house of words, songs, thoughts?* There is none to ask. Yet he couldn't stop his mind from returning back to her reflection skewed in scarlet blood, her neck cut by a knife like a chicken, blood spotting her lemon green dress, her creamy white shoes, her sage green handbag.

Because he circled her casket like everyone else was doing that doesn't mean that he knew what he was doing.

When they finished goodbyes, and when he had swallowed his quite goodbyes in his heart they sang songs for her again. He sang along to the sounds that still lied deep within him, to the sounds that he knew would never restrict him again. Some people sang songs to console themselves. He sang the same songs to control. Some people sang songs to release, to please, too intense and strange to add to his discomfort. He just sang along to those stone-skipping songs, defeating his hallucinations. His face would jerk into life, here and there, when an untuned note echoed off their creaky notes. The breezy wind was lifting those hymns to lurch and swoop all over the grave place.

Tiny tufts of invalid clouds left over by those small clicks of rain that had shivered on their way to the graveyards were like the minister who seemed so lonely- so far away- as they were both ministering an unheard sermon. The minister was not speaking from the heart about mend and glory but was using a scripted speech that had nothing to do with Lillian. The late afternoon twilight exposed the sky's godless blue, such blue was shouting in the skies.

The breezy wind was playing with the dropped decaying leaves of the fig tree's disrobing like a child playing alone. Every restless leaf was a restless soul, hustled and bustled in the wind and, the wind was scattering slowly the leaves around and about to the westerly direction. Scattering the smell of death around the grave place since this westerly breezy wind was scented sickly sweet with the miasma of Lillian and her grave tidings.

The five or so crows, on top of the nearby shrub of pucker trees to the east taunted and squawked their own supposed twenty-one gun salute. Their sharp notes surfed the wind. They had a feel for rhythm and an ear for sound repetition. One of the crows flew away as if something out there called it. Its shadow staining sunbright heads below with something darker, a smell of something primal, something naked, raw…, a wail of unbelieving loss. Don kept following its flight in the skies. It kept calling out and the other four crows followed through. He didn't know where they were herding towards, maybe there were herding to another grave place; to do another of their gun salutes. When he had lost those crows into the expanding skies, he looked down from the sky. The grave men were now lowering Lillian into the grave.

He thought he hadn't seen well, and then he looked again. Yes, they were lowering Lillian's casket down into the grave. When he saw her being lowered down into the grave that's when he really started to think that all along that he hadn't been dreaming. It really was happening. He had lost her to the dust just like he had lost his parents twenty four years before. When his parents died, he didn't know what to do. He was a child, he supposed, he couldn't have done anything, really. He hadn't cried when his foster parent died in his last year at the University. He just didn't have tears for him! He wasn't going to cry now. He might have turned out a weeping male wreck if he started on it. *To be private in a public place was rare self possession,* he psyched himself.

He had also been given to think that it was better to harden into granite than to soften into powder but he wished for the ground on which he stood to just open up and let him inside it and then cover him from this loss.

Someone outside the grave lifted up a stone whilst someone inside the grave signalled, caught the stone and lowered it into the grave to layer it on top of the casket of Lillian, to protect her from the soil, from instant decay. Lillian's casket was deeper inside a smaller grave hole inside the bigger grave hole, so this stone was layered on the ledge that separated these two parts of the grave, and then the soil would come on top of this layer of stones. The stone spawned silence as the children and women started to leave this grave place. Leaving the men to burry Lillian! Don could not only know those boulders of stones as stones, he also could tell them as sadness.

He wished the grave they had lowered Lillian into could have demanded for him, by refusing to be filled up by the soil. He could have entered it, happily. No! The grave started playing hide and seek with him only that he never found out anything from it. The grave started laughing deviously at him as they were filling it up with the dark grey clay soils by lengthening.

Even when they were filling it up, it lengthened, lengthened by the spirit puddles of those damp cloths of rain that had drizzled on their way to the graveyards, over an hour before. The grave continued lengthening; lengthened by the spirits that had been hidden by the Priest's ecclesiastical pomp and the singer's circumstantial songs. The grave's laughter lengthened, all around this grave place and, it lengthened from the people's muted groans, their silent cries and even by the silence now at this grave place. It didn't even stop laughing, lengthening in laughter, as the noise of the soil, as it was hitting the bottom of her grave and the grave-men's silent talk and signals. The grave kept lengthening; it lengthened, as the heaviness of the earth in mid-summer, thick as cake. And the wind kicked up, swirling brute facts back and forth across this grave place.

The grave started making fun at him. He felt it starting to mock him. It started challenging him.

It said, and it's only him who heard it.

"I have triumphed over you man by taking Lillian away from you and leaving you with nothing, what do you really have now?" In another moment it said, nonchalantly.

"There is no need for me to hurry up my closure, stupid; did you think you deserved anything, really, fool!" It said to him that it was now like the trees around this grave place. It was here to live forever. That even at that, trees were exceptional people, not like humans, not like him. They lose their leaves without such a fuss, they stay at the same place all their lives, do not ask for anything, any favours, and never bothered anyone. They just accepted what was there for the taking.

"But the sun isn't waiting for you, fool." Then it cackled in laughter as the evening started hugging the trees by staring out between the shivers of leaves. The long lines of images haunting the late afternoon hours, and the afternoon hours were now a glimmering filament waving at the sun. The tall sprawling Mopani trees, and the three poplar trees hunched like three old men and the hulk of the baobab tree some distances from the grave place, to the western side, started to yield a schema: consuming a role, in dancing with the fading daylight, he realised that he could never really cover the grave's challenging laughter and stare.

When he realised the grave they had lowered Lillian into could never convince him that she was really dead he left this grave place, all alone, for the small forest nearby. He knew that deep down his heart he had not encased Lillian in the soils. She hadn't crumbled into dust, that he still hadn't buried her. He had refused to bury her by leaving this grave-place for the forest. It was all a lie; there had been no corpse but two dissected parts that seemed like were of Lillian. There had been no coffin, not even a grave that he could see. His million whys had no goodbyes, no answers? They hadn't been any farewell. They had been no song, no sermon, no flower, and no departing hour under the Mubvaropa tree. To which he could even add his own unshed tears, corroding the bottoms of his eye sockets with their want to be let out. He couldn't let them out, even though they were killing him, destroying his eyesight.

The Lillian that he loved was still touching his shoulder like the westerly wind, so there was no need to cry for her, when she was still that alive in the wind. She was still calling his name. They were still expecting their first son together. Lillian was still dreaming with him even as he was traversing this small forest. He still felt the laughter of his first son echoing in the voices in his heart. He refused to accept he had attended a funeral. He could never end this chapter.

I know I have to rehearse at forgetting so as to let her go!

He walked and walked until he was lost in this small forest. Thinking he should retrace his footsteps, but he hadn't left any footmarks to follow back out of this forest, so he started wondering up and down the dales of this forest and gaze about, unseeing; plodding the little ways off the old logging road, runaway thoughts blaring in his head like a stuck car horn. These unleashed thoughts were cropping powerlessly over the treed forest.

In the seeded speckle of light the night was glowing with pinpricks of misunderstanding, the lightness of the dark pressed him against the land so he couldn't really fly with the wind. Marram grass was whispering, calling him with a discourse of the saints. He was seeing this grass flattening in loops like two dogs running fast. One shrill note set black crowned night herons loose from the Mango trees, a murder of wings silencing the amassing whispering sounds of Marram grass. The only other sound he heard was that of the dried listless leaves, alive to every stirring of the wind; the wind garlanding wordlessness around his throat. It was only the wind that he could measure himself by.

By the time he found his way through all the countrified roads of this small forest, to the graveplace again, it was dark. It wasn't that dark, though, because the sky had three moons. One was a dark halo, the halo that was inside him. The other one was the colour of milk, a creamy milky colour. The third one was orangey-red, a thirsty orangey-red, but all the three moons were shinning a faint trail of light as the moons were moving with him, even as he was plodding the forest. Sometimes the moons were a black halo, sometimes milky, sometimes orangey-red, sometimes so small and, he was trying to catch up with those three moons; grim, ungraceful, gargantuan things.

When he returned back to the graveplace he knew he had returned for a certain purpose. He hadn't really been lost all the time he was plodding in the small forest. He had been on his way to this graveplace. The forest acted as a place one could go to be alone but that it had also become a place he had gone to be alone in a certain way. Something was reinforced when he was in that forest. He had become like Orpheus who risked going into the underworld to

61

retrieve the woman he loved. Though he still didn't know the answers he had gone to forest to figure out; for the answers he knew were not the answers. He had eaten through the answers already. He should have gone there to learn the questions. Now he had returned back to the graveplace to do exactly that.

Turning back to this grave place was now the most interesting thing he had ever done in his life. He would now face the grave with a sure truth. The truth was; he was imagining lifting her back out of this page of the earth that had encased her. It was ridiculous to still be thinking Lillian could be negotiated for over and through the soil, yet it's exactly what he had returned back to do.

The late evening birds, sorrowful birds, woefully sad singers, had retreated into the night's receding darkness. They had given up on him with their commentary and chatter, slapping time, a staccato riff on a darkening sky beat. Listening intently to their voices he heard dissonance, of a doubtful drummer. It didn't help him some because it couldn't shift the effect of this undesirable that was inside him into indecipherable.

Two Owls entered the proceedings, an orchestra apologising for not sensing death all along, hanging their thoughts on the moon's nook. In their music they created a bluesy note, a darker bluesy note expanding, deepening the other evening birds' song- the owls' thudding hoot of angry blood demanding for vengeance, rumbling, *"It never rains for you"*, *"what are you going to do,"* *"it never rains for you,"* *"blood for blood,"* *"it never rains for you,"* *"what are going to do?"*. The music was there in the songs but the words were lost to the wind, except for the rhythms. *"It never rains for you"*, *"what are you going to do,"* *"it never rains for you,"* *"blood for ...."*

He came to the lower side of Lillian's grave and sat down by his haunches. The night had made nest in the hallow of her grave and her killed scent had been killed by the miasmas of the packed grave. The hallow curve of the grave was speechless. He touched the soil of Lillian's grave with his two hands in order to really be sure that the grave was really there. The mound was there. He remembered it had been a monumental effort that had rolled that grave up. Her grave was now a blonde expanse pock-marked with giblets like hail on the landscape. This fresh mound was casting eerie shadows pockmarked by the shadows of the halo moon. It was obvious that she had left the land blank and that, she had scribed on it.

Don didn't want to think that someday a tree would grow on top of Lillian's grave or something else like weeds or roses, perhaps. These- feeding on her love; getting all the nourishment from Lillian's body that was now being denied to him.

I must create ancient Mexican premature and miscarried bebes into clay look-alikes using Lillian's grave soils for ritual returning, he thought. Ceramic and ash Lillians to hold in his hands, not to bury in the graves as had happened to Lillian. Or he could have buried her with a small painted alabaster stature like the ancient Egyptians did. In fact he could have created two of these and, he would have kept one for himself. This ushtabi would help her doing work in the afterlife, so also him in this life. They would have a lot of time together, he thought. Now he was alone. He knew he would be alone for the rest of his life, maybe he would be buried with a mouse as ancient bachelors were buried with in Zimbabwe, for accompaniment in afterlife. His own body was a warehouse of pain. He wished the tears could be made to flow from his eyes to make a sea so that this grave could be touched and be swept away from existence by the tears.

He couldn't help asking his wife and child where they were now.

"Where are your skulls, what is my sin?" He groaned the question without real words coming out.

And Lillian seemed to shine through the grave like a brilliant wreckage of his broken dreams. Smiling at him, the planet whose gravity he now orbited, tugging at his shores, telling him that.

"Life doesn't owe its serenity to such impatience. You are broken, Don; you have to go for repairs, home." These tread tides of sentences nearly drawn in words that even ancestors couldn't speak.

Telling him that the pain's real home was not to be there with her but to be with the living; he had to let her go so that she could find rest where she was. He accepted her admonishments and advice. He left for the sanctuary of the living. He returned home with the gun that he had been carrying on him for days. He hadn't buried the gun with Lillian. This gun was more than an ushtabi, a mouse, or an ash Lillian for Don. It represented the hunger and hurt that stayed inside him. He will never give it back.

His face was etched with a new darkness, so exhausting. He had been buried with someone. The sky above was painted a purplish night blue. As he left the grave place the insane light of those moth-eaten half moons were throwing shadows on the grave, bleaching the grave, leaving it ancient, softer, flatter, bluing in the dusk. And a general purpling was on the western skies as the fading amber light of the moons send him homebound. It was still on the twenty sixth, late evening; that those moons were now sending him homebound.

Prologue: Servants of the Rice
A novel extract
... In which a decision in made
By Audrey McCombs (USA)

Antananarivo, 1828

The king is dying. He will be dead. Perhaps a week, perhaps less. And no one else knows.

Ramavo emerges from the Tranovola into the northern courtyard of the palace compound. The silver bells that hang from the Silver House fill the air with their silver song. Ramavo stands at the threshold, listening, and her skin tingles as if dusted with silver chimes. The notes are small, but like small things they slip into the cracks of the world. The silver is in the air itself, suspended in the spaces between the light, it surrounds her, carries past her and as she looks out to the west the whole city of Antananarivo is infused with silver. An inhale, an exhale, and the silver swirls, assembles, twists into filaments that cross and connect as the strands of a great web. The web that tunnels through the interstices of the world.

Ramavo stands at the center of the web and fingers the trembling strands, listens to the ringing reverberations with her skin and her feet and the pumping of her blood. She listens to the lemurs perched in the treetops one hundred miles away, masticating, slurping, spitting seeds; to the precise pitch of the drongo's call, black ventriloquist king; to the sighs of leaf geckos immobile and invisible on the trunks of the trees. She listens to the tickling of butterfly wings. To the lightness of the air at the front of a storm descending on Tamatave. To the rasp of sharpening steel in Ikongo. To the padding feet of a stranger carrying a secret on his back. To the scolding of a farmer to his son. Ramavo hears the quick movements of hands exchanging goods for silver piastres. The rubbing of honey onto a holy idol. The fingering of an ody bag on a string around a neck. The debate of noble men. And always, underneath everything, Ramavo feels the undulating rice, like a rolling foundation upon which all else turns.

Ramavo raises her hand above her head as if she were pulling a thread from her spindle, and she listens to the web of the world thrum in response. Ramavo's fingers speak their secret to the web, strumming the strands that reach forward to her progeny, backward to her ancestors. This thing that she knows, it resonates and the whole world answers, reverberating. She knows what no one else knows. The king is dying.

Radama will be dead. Perhaps a week, perhaps less.

The gate from the north courtyard to the south is as smooth under her hand as if it had been dipped in molten silver, and as cold. Ahead of her, from between two of the crowded houses she hears more bells, but it is only women's laughter. As she closes the gate the women appear—it is the king's favorite wife, the foreigner Rasalimo, still young and pretty and wearing her Sakalava salovana tucked up under her large, still-firm breasts. Her matching blue kisaly cloaks her hair and drapes her shoulders and her face is painted today, *mason'droany* again, yellow and white swirls and stars for a festival the Merina don't celebrate. The woman has never been comfortable in the Merina capital, part hostage, part wife, but the one time she escaped it turned out badly, and so she stays and surrounds herself with laughing women so she herself is relieved of the duty. But she laughs when she sees Ramavo, the cast-aside first wife trying to enliven her dull hair and tired skin and old eyes with gaudy French satin.

Rasalimo laughs when she sees Ramavo. Always before the favorite's laugh has been a silver knife slicing sideways under the first wife's skin, flaying her at intervals, but today the knife disintegrates under the force of Ramavo's knowing, falls like dust at Ramavo's feet, and Ramavo looks down onto the swept dirt of the courtyard expecting to see a mound of laughing silver powder and when she doesn't she looks up at Rasalimo in surprise. The king's favorite is confused, then dismissive as she and her women turn without a word and glide to the south gate and out of the palace compound. In a moment not infused with silver it would have been a slap in the face, the younger women not greeting the old, the junior wife not greeting the senior. But Ramavo's knowledge is shield and armor, sword and spear, gunpowder in a firing cannon, and in this moment the pretty young woman is just a girl who used to be favored by a king.

The king is dying. He will be dead.

Ramavo walks back to her house just to the north of the Besakana. The Tranovola, the Silver House, has been Radama's seat of power because it impresses the Europeans, but before Radama the great King Andrianampoinimerina used the Besakana for affairs of state. The Besakana is ancient, and sacred, and empty now. Ramavo does not enter her house, but pokes her head in the door and calls to her two sister wives, Rabodomirahalahy and Rasendrasoa. They follow her to the Besakana, and Ramavo and her sisters begin preparing rice and a thin *kabaka*, nominally to take to the ailing king.

The voices of Rabodomirahalahy and Rasendrasoa strip some of the charge from the air, and the hairs on the back of Ramavo's arms are beginning to lie back down as she rolls out a tsihy mat and sits down on it to think. Rasendrasoa, tossing rice in a *sahafa* to separate out the rocks, asks her *How is the king?* And Ramavo almost answers. She almost says, but she does not. In her nose still hangs metallic blood, putrid and moldy flesh, and toward the king creeps a shadow of ebony that has touched but not yet enveloped him. It will. Soon.

Perhaps a week, perhaps less. And no one else knows.

He is attended in his illness by his royal guard, the *tsimandos,* who are strong and loyal and stupid. The only death they know is the death delivered in battle. They do not know that a man can also die of too much drink and too many women. But Ramavo knows this. The daughter of a Merina prince, Ramavo has lived her life among nobles—her uncle also died this way. Ramavo attended him in his descent and still remembers the taste of death delivered by gluttony.

In Radama's room she swallowed and swallowed but still the taste would not leave her tongue.

On the *tsihy* mat she gathers branches of cassava and begins to strip the leaves. Normally she would boil the leaves then pound them into a paste, but today she makes food for a dying king, and so the broth will be thin and only lightly salted. Her fingers work automatically, twisting then pulling the leaves from the stems, and the pile of leaves at her side grows without her even noticing.

Ramavo remembers as a child attending the great *kabarys* of King. Andrianampoinimerina, when the entire population of Imerina would gather in the square of Andohalo to hear the king speak. She sat with her aunts and she could always find her father among the other noble men, his scarlet *lamba* shining with more silver, his place always close to the king. She remembers peanuts roasted with salt and sugar, and the old king's voice like the great River Ikopa watering the plains of Betsimitatatra. Feeding the rice fields, feeding the people, growing huge and angry when the ancestors were offended warm and playful when there was a story to be told. Twenty thousand Merina when Ramavo was a child, every one of them embraced and scolded and educated by the great King Andrianampoinimerina.

Ten years later, when Radama was newly king and still would suffer her at his side, the square at Andohalo filled with soldiers to receive the blessing of the *sampy*. She remembers the smell of twenty thousand iron spears like a lake of blood at his feet, and the taste of male lust choking her like musk. Radama expanded the territories of Imerina until his kingdom could no long fit into the square at Andohalo, so he ruled with his armies and the guns he bought with his treaty with the English. Who would have thought such a thin and flimsy thing as a piece of paper could hold such power over the King of Imerina?

To succeed him, Radama named his daughter as soon as she was born. She is to marry his teenage nephew when she comes of age, and though he says she will have sole sovereign power, everyone knows they will rule together, or she will be ruled by her husband. Everyone thinks the issue moot for many years to come. Now, Ramavo imagines the girl child wobbling on the sacred stone of Andohalo, the citizens of Imerina straining to hear a voice that is too young and too small to carry past the first row of nobles. Ramavo knows the king's nephew, who loves the paper of the English missionaries better than he loves the spears and guns of his father. She imagines him at the head of an army and almost laughs out loud at this vision of bumbling chaos.

Rabodomirahalahy and Rasendrasoa do not notice her silent snort—they are busy fanning the charcoal to start the rice fire burning. They gossip about Rasalimo, the favorite wife, about the strange Sakalava taboos she refuses to abandon even though she is married and should properly adopt the customs of her husband. Rasalimo has not been kind to Rabodomirahalahy or Rasendrasoa, and now is burnt by the fire she herself kindled.

Ramavo hates Rasalimo for hating her position, because Rasalimo has the ear of the king but refuses to speak. If Ramavo could speak, she would say a great many things. She would tell the king that the English are using him—that they feed him alcohol and feed him women and he does exactly what they want him to do. Radama is a weak king controlled by his lusts. Ramavo has her own lusts, this she knows. She loves thick, fatty beef *kabaka,* chicken stewed with mangoes, dried fish from Tamatave fried in oil and mashed with goose eggs. She loves her satin in all the colors of the *vanga,* and her coral comb and gold and silver bracelets that spark like lightening when she moves.

But Ramavo is smart where Radama is not. All the king understands is his own desire, for women and for war. Ramavo grew up at the market; she understands the bartering game, that the first person to name a price loses. Andriamihaja taught her the foreign writing while he was wooing her, and now she understands about taxes and trade. She knows where Radama's rice comes from, and she would bet her coral comb that the king does not.

But Radama is dying. He will be dead, in a week, maybe less. His heirs are not fit to rule, and the two factions at court will fight for control until the conquered tribes—the Betsileo, the Bezanozano, the Betsimisaraka, the Betanimena—have all thrown off Merina rule, and with it Merina taxes, and Imerina will once again be an impoverished Sakalava vassal state. She, Ramavo, will lose her rice fields, her coral comb, her silks and satins, her cattle, her loom, her perfumes, her shoes, and her home.

The Besakana is filling with smoke from the fire, and Rabodomirahalahy and Rasendrasoa are scolding each other for improperly setting the stove. The cassava leaves smell bitter, and the stem she holds is sharp at one end from the machete's cut. Ramavo presses the point into the pad of her left middle finger. She hardly feels the pain and watches the red bead grow, then grow bigger than itself and spill down the side of her finger. How many times has she fantasized about reigning in Imerina? Imagined herself holding the scepter and wearing the heavy gold crown? She has always wondered about its weight, wondered how long she could wear it and still hold her head high. She has thought carefully about how she could use the English paper, so full of power, to rule.

How many times? Hundreds of times. Thousands. Every time Radama placates the English, every time the missionaries preach: the ancestors are powerless and must be forgotten. Every time Rasalimo laughs at her: Ramavo humiliated, forgotten. Every time she is silent when she feels she must scream. Thousands of times. Tens of thousands. She and Andriamihaja have made a bedroom game of it. He likes it better when he is king, but she likes it better when he is just her lover. He calls her Ranavalona during these games, "the one kept to the side."

And now the king is dying. He will be dead. His heirs are not fit to reign, and she will lose what little she has.

70

Ranavalona would be a better ruler than Radama ever was.

Ranavalona curses and sticks her finger in her mouth, sucking at the blood. Rasendrasoa looks up from the bubbling rice and asks what has happened. Ranavalona stares at her, then tells her it's nothing, just a scratch. The cassava leaves are stripped and ready for boiling. Rasendrasoa looks at Ranavalona, her puzzled expression a mirror of Rasalimo's before her. Ranavalona stands up from her place on the tsihy mat. She is distracted. She must see Andriamihaja. She mutters about her finger to Rabodomirahalahy and Rasendrasoa, who protest, *What about the king's rice?* But she is already out the door. At the last second she turns and tells them they must not visit the king until she returns. Then she is gone. There is need for haste.

Ranavalona knows that Andriamihaja is ambitious. The whole kingdom knows this about him. She has never asked herself what portion of Andriamihaja's attentions are for her, and what portion are for himself. She has always ignored the whispers—what good would such a question serve? But now she has her own question for him, one that demands an answer. And she hurries to his house to ask.

The king is dying. He will be dead. How far will Andriamihaja go to advance his own interests?

She will offer him great expanses of rice fields. She will offer to make him Prime Minister, and Commander-in-Chief of the army. She will offer him *tsy maty manota*, an exemption from capital punishment no matter what his crimes.

Later, when he suggests they enlist Andriamamba, Ranavalona lets him think it was his own idea.

Okwu n'eso Akuko: Odibo Osikapa

By Audrey McCombs (USA)

Translated into Igbo by Gabriel Egboluche

Antananarivo, 1828

Onwu ezuola eze ahu. O nwere ike ikubi mgbe obula. Onwere ike ibu n'otu izu m'obu n'abali ole n'ole. Onweghi onye ma mgbe o ga-abu.

Ramavo siri n'obi eze puta n'ama were lebe anya n'ugwu. O nara nti were nu uda mgbirimgba ola ocha na-aku egwu mara mma. Egwu si na mgbirimgba a ada wuru ya akpata oyi. Uda ya di ala mana omere ka Ramavo chikota onwe ya were chee echiche ndu ya. Mgbirimgba a were akuko ndu ya, chee ya n'ihu. Dika oja eji agbara oha obodo ama, uda mgbirimgba a ruturu nsotu Antananarivo nile, were uso egwu ya dee ya uri ma jikota kwa uwa nile onu.

Ka Ramavona-achighari ihe omimi ndia n'obi ya, akpata oyi zuru ya ahu. Ahu ya na-ama jijiji ka onye zutere ndi mmuo. Orunyere onwe ya nile n'uda egwu a, uche ya wee puo n'erughari.

Obi Ramavo gara n'ube umu enwe n'amaghari n'elu osisi ebe ha no na-ata nri. Ha taa, ha loo ma gboputa kwa ya, mee onu ka aguu ogbuola ha. O nukwara osu nwa ngwere no n'elu osisi, na mkpotu nku irukurububa na-efeghari na-eme.

Ihe ndia nile wee di ya ka onye mmiri onuru toro n'eze. O dikwa ya ka ikuku oma agu ifufe na egbe eluigwe na eso n'azu. Di ya ka uda obejiri ana amu n'igwe, na uda ukwu onye obia mkpumkpu kwaputara n'azu. O dikwa ya ka aka-na-nti dinta doro nwa oru ya. Di ya ka nwagbogho zutere muona nduru uzo. Dikwa nwa dibia emnyere ihere. Mana odighi etu a. Kama, o bu, nkarita uka ndi nze. Nke a mere Ramavo jiri kwere n'obi ya na awo adighi agba oso ehihie na nkiti.

Ramavo welitere aka ya elu ka o na acho itupusi owu ojiri kee isi ya n'obi onuma. Iwe no ya n'obi ruru ala ndi mmuo. Izuzu nani ya ma, ejula ya isi. O ji ngwugwu nani ya ma ihe no ya n'ime. N'onwu na-achosi eze ike, bu ngwugwu nani ya ma ebe esiri kesi ya.

Radama no n'onu onwu. Onwere ike inwu n'otu izu m'obu n'ubochi ole n'ole.

Site n'onu uzo ukwu nke chebere ihu n'ugwu ruo na ndida, obi eze dika ebe eliri ozu gbasaa. Ka o gara nso ebe ulo obibi ndi nwuye eze ndi ozo no, onuru uda ochi ha. Tupu omechie onuzo, nwunye eze nke di eze n'obi, Rasalimo, duru umunwayi ndi odibo ya puta. Eze lutara Rasalimo na mba ozo. O ka bu nwata, ndu na mma zuru ahu. Okere ukwu akwa ya ma tinye ha n'okpurunnukwu ara ya abuo kwu gem n'elu obi ya. Nnukwu ichafu ojiri kpuchie isi na ubu ya n'acha anunu anunu wee masi ukwu akwa oma n'ukwu ya. Odere uri n'ihu ka onye na-aga mmemme na mba Merina.

Raslimo ji afufu na onu biri na Melina. N'ezie, obu nwunye eze, mana ihe ozo bu n'odi ya k'ono na mkporo. Anya di ya n'ama. Otutu ugboro ka ochoro ihapu onodu ya dika nwunye eze. Mana ugboro ole ahu ka eze gwara ya na anaghi ata nti ya ata. Iji machie uwa jooji, ochoro umunwayi ndi odi ka odi ya, wee gbaa onwe ya gburugburu. Ha na-akparita onwe ha obi oma.

Mana mgbe obula ohuru Ramavo, bu nwunye eze nke mbu, nke eze n'anaghi elezi anya, ochi n'eju Rasalimo onu.

Ihe a n'ewute Ramavo nke ukwuu. Mana taa, Ramavo huru ihe k'ubi wee ree oba. Ihe no ya n'obi bu uru maka ihe omara banyere eze. Nke a kariri ochi Rasalimo chiri ya. O leturu anya n'ala tupu owelite ihu wee kuo Raslimo anya mmute. Nke a gbanwojuru Raslimo anya, mana obiaghi chigharia ya n'obi ya. Kama, o sitere n'uzo di na ugwu ama wee puoro onwe ya.Obughi ma ihe Ramavo mara banyere eze, o kara iputa uka na nwunye eze oburu uzo bia ije di, huru ya ma ghara ikele ya. O leghara ya anya, kpoo ya obere nwa jiri mberede baa eze n'obi.

Eze no n'onu onwu. Onwere ike igbabi n'otu izu m'obu ubochi ole n'ole.

73

Ramavo laghachiri be ya n'ugwu nke Beskana. Eze jiri Tranovola, nke bu ulo ola ocha, were mere obi maka na omasiri ndi ocha ndi siri Europe bia obodo Melina. Mana tupu Radama achiba, eze amara aha ya bu Igweh Andrianampoinimerina jiri Besakana mere obi ya. Besakana bu ulo ochie di omimi.N'agbanyeghi na enweghi onye bi na ya ugbua, ugwu zuru ya ahu.

Ramavo lebara anya n'uzo wee kpoo ndi nwuye-di ya abuo ndi ozo, Rabodomirahalahy and Rasendrasoa. Ha soro ya gaa na Beskana ebe ha ga ano wee sie osikapa na kabaka ha ga ebugara eze.

Ka ha na akwado nri, Olu nkarita uka nke Rabodomirahalahy and Rasendrasoa medara Ramavo obi, were wepu echiche ya ebe oria eze no. O were ute tuo n'ala nodi n'akuku ebe Rasendrasoa na afuchasi osikapa, ma burukwa isi ya n'aka. "Kedu ka eze mere," Rasendrasoa juru ya. Ramavo choro iza ya ma onu kuchiri ya. O bi ya gara ebe eze no ozo. O di ka ochichi n'erughari n'obi eze. Ochichi a nwere ike ikpuchi eze. N'ezie, o ga-ekpuchi ezemgbe na-adighi anya, bu ihe ogwara onwe ya. Nkea doro ya anya.

Onwere ike buru otu izu m'obu abali ole n'ole. Odighi onye mara mgbe o ga-abu.

Umu odibo eze n'ele ya oria. Ha bu umuokorobia ndu juru onu. Obi ha no n'oru ha na-aru, mana ako n'uche esoghi ha noro oru a. Asi na ha mara ihe, ha ga ama na onwu abughi soso mgbe egburu mmadu n'ihu agha. Onwu no na mmanya noro kwa n'ukwu umunwayi, Ramavo chere n'obi ya.

O mara nkea maka n'obu nwa okpara eze nke Merina. O toro n'etiti ndi amuru n'obi eze. O chetara na nwanne nna ya nwuru udi onwu a. Onwu oke ochicho, oke nri na amaghi ihe na-ebute.

Ramavo were osisi akpu ochikotara n'ugbo bido na-akpacha aku ya. O kwesiri isu ha n'ikwe mana ebe obu nri eze ka eji ha esi, o ga-ebe ha ebe, tinye ya nnu ma were ha siere eze ofe. Nwa obere oge, o kpachara nnukwu aku akpu karia etu otubara anya.

Ramavo chetara mgbe o na-eso ebunye ndi nze na onowu eze nri na mmanya na be nna ya. Ihe a na-abu mgbe obula enwere ogbako ndi oha n'eze n'obi eze. O na-eso umunwanne mama ya nodu ala mgbe obula eze na-agwa ndi o na-achi okwu. O na-echeta ebe nna ya na ano n'etiti ndi ichie, yiri ola ozo na-amuke amuke n'ukwu ya. Nna ya na-anodebe eze nso. O na-echetakwa ukpala ejiri nnu na oto biribiri were ghee, nke ana-eke n'obi eze. Olu eze na-adi ka iyi Ikpoba nke na enye ala nile ndu ma mee ka ihe akoro n'ubi too. N'agbanye gi ntamu otutu ndi mmadu, eze diri elekota obodo ya nile anya n'uzo kwesiri ekwesi.

Mana mgbe afo iri na agala, Radama aghoola eze. Ramavo hukwara onwe ya n'akuku ya. O na-cheta uda mma na egbe nke Eze Radama jiri chia ndi obodoya. Igwe ndi aha ya siri ike. Ojiri ha luso obodo nile no ya nso ogu wee merie ha ma kporo ha tinyere ndi o na-achi. O mubara ala Merina nke na obi ya enwezighi ike iba ubara mmadu o na-achi. O jiri aka ike, ndi agha na egbe ozutara n'aka ndi ocha si obodo England were nyuo ndi o na-achi anya. O binyekwara aka n'otutu akwukwo ndi ocha nyere ya. Onweghi onye mara na aka ndia eze binyere n'akwukwo ga-emechaa nwee nnkuwu ike n'ebe eze no. Akwkukwo ndia mechara juo eze muo chiri ya ozo.

Mgbe amutaara ya nwada, Eze Ramada egbugi oge ihoputa ya ka oburu onye ga-achi Merina ma achoo ya ahughi.Ogbara mbo ihu na ada ya luru nwa nwanne ya nke nwoke. N'agbanyeghi na eze kwuru n'obu ada ya ga eji ike nile, odoro ndi mmadu anya na obu di ya ga achi. Ojokata njo, ha n'abuo achi ba.

Mana oruo la n'omume. Ramavo na-eche otu nwata nwanyi a ga-esi ebu ibu ochichi Merina n'isi. Otu o ga-esi achikota oha mmadu nile onu. Nke ka njo buna di ya, bu nwa nwanne eze, abughi onye omenala na-amasi. O bu nwata huru ndu ndi ocha n'anya ma chee na ogu enweghi onodu n'ebe mmadu no. Mgbe obula Ramavo chetara n'obu onye a ga-edu ndi agha nke Merina, o na-eri ya onu.

Rabodomirahalahy na Rasendrasoa no na afu oku ha ji esi osikapa. Nkea mere n'obi ha adighi n'ebe Ramavo no. Mgbe ha nwere ohere, ha na-asi asiri banyere Rasalimo, bu nwunye nke eze huru n'anya. O na-ewute ha na nwada a si mba ozo achoghi ime omenala nke di ya. Kama, o ka na-eme omume ejiri mara ndi be nna ya. Nke jogburu onwe ya na njo bu na Rasalimo echieela Rabodomirahalahy na Rasendrasoa onu n'ala. O doro anya na egwu Rasalimo kubara ka o ga-agba mgbe na-adighi anya.

Otu n'he mereRamavo jiri kpoo Rasalimo asi bu na Rasalimo ejighi onodu ya dika nwunye eze huru n'anya kporo ihe. N'agbanyeghi na eze na-ege ya nti, o naghi adu eze odu obula. O buru na Rasalimo maara ihe, o ka agwa eze otutu ihe ga-abara obodo uru. O ka agwa eze na ndi ocha si England ji ya eme akaje. Ha nye ya mmanya, ha akponye ya umuagbogho, o na-eso ha ka ewu. Radama bu eze n'efe anu ahu ya. Ramavo makwa na ya nwa nwekwara ebe osi eri mperi nke ya. O mara na o jighi anu ehi, okuko, azu okpoo amiri na mmanu Tamatave egwu egwu. O hukwara uwe ya na ihe ndi oji ejikwa onwe yan'anya.

Mana ihe di iche bu na Ramavo ma ihe Radama na-amaghi.O nwere amaihe eji azu ahia, mara na onye buru uzo juo anya, emegbuo ya. O makwara asu oyibo. Nwoke anakpo Andriamihaja kuziere ya ide oyibo oge nwokorobia na-acho ka ha yia. O makwa gbasara ugwo utu isi nke ndi oha obodo na atu nye ndi ochichi.

Radama no n'onu onwu. O nwere ike inwu n'izu a ma obu n'izu ozo.

Ndi n'eso ya enweghi nke nwere ike eji achi obodo. Ha akpurula onwe ha gaa n'ulo ikpe. Ha nwere ike ino n'ulo ewu amu o n'ogbu. Ha aghaghi ino n'ulo ikpe ruo mgbe ndi mba nile Eze Radma lutara n'ogu - ndi Betsileo, Bezanozano, Betsimisaraka naBetanimenaga-gbuhara isi onwe ha, wee kwusi ikwu ugwo utu isi nye Merina. Obodo Merina ga-abiazi buru ulo aguu n'ala Sakalava. Mgbe ahu, ugbo osikapa Ramavo, ga-efunaghi ya.

Anwuru oku ejula onu ulo nile. Rabodomirahalahy, m'obu Rasendrasoa akwanyeghi ekwe oku ha ji esi nri ofuma. Ha no na ata onwe ha uta maka ya. Ramavo were otu onu nke osisi oji n'aka were nwayoo dupuo onwe ya ahu.

O noro na-eche ugboro ole omasiri ya ichi obodo Imerina. O na-eche otu o ga-adi ma oyiri okpu eze nke uhie, noro n'oche eze na enye ntuzi aka. O no na-eche udi aru okpu eze ga-adi, na afo ole onwere ike ikpu ya tupu ochichi ya agwu. O no na-che etu o ga-esi ede ihe n'akwukwo nke ga enyekwu ya ike o ga-eji were chia.

Ugboro ole? Otutu ugboro, k'ozara onwe ya n'obi ya. Mgbe nile Eze Radama mere ka omeedaa ndi ocha England obi, oge nile ohapuru ndi ocha n'agbasa ozioma n'ala Merina,ndi mmuo na ndi egede nwe obodo Merina na adi ka ndi echefuru echefu. Mgbe obula Rasalimo chiri ya ochi, Ramavo na enwe nwute dika onye echefuru echefu. Mgbe obula ogbara nkiti, o di ya ka ya tie mkpu. Otutu ugboro, nnukwuru nnu ugboro. Ya na Andriamihaja na-achighari ihea mgbe nile ha no n'ime ulo.

Mana ugbua, onwu no eze nso. O ga-anwu mgbe n'adighi aanya. Ndi nnochi anya ya enweghi nke ochichi doro anya. Nke ojoo bu na ya nwa bu Ramavo ga-atufu obere ihe onwere

Ranavalona gara achita ofuma karia otuRadama nwere ike isi chi a.

Ranavalona mara osu were mkpuru aka ya tinye n'onu na-ami obara n'agbaputa na ya.

Rasendrasoa weliri anya n'osikapa o na-esi wee juo ya ihe mere ya mana osara na o bu obere onya omehiara onwe ya. Okwesiri ka Ranavalona tinye akwukwo akpu n'ite osikapa mana o meghi ya. Ka ma obulitere n'ute ya, ka onye ihe juru isi wee puo, n'agbanyeghi na nri eze di n'oku.Ravanlona doro ha aka na nti ka ha ghara I ga ebe eze no ruo mgbe ya lotara ebe o na-aga. Rasendrasoa lere Ranavalona anya wee hu omume Rasalimo ozigbo. Ha juru ya ihe aga eme nri eze. Mana tupu ha ajuchaa,o puolari.

Ranavalona mara na Andriamihaja nwere oke ochicho ka ya. Obodo nile mara nkea banyere ya. Mana o doghi ya anya ihe o choro n'aka ya. O jube ghi ajuju mana o choputala mkpa odi imata ihe o nwere ike inweta ma oburu na Andriamihaja nweta ihe ona acho. Ojiri ije oso gaba na be ya.

Eze no n'onu onwu. O ga-anwu mgbe na-adighi anya. Kedu ihe Andiamihaja nwere ike ime iji nweta ihe o na-acho?

Ochere n'onwe ya sina ya ga enye Andiamihaja ugbo osikapa buru ibu. O ga-eme ya Onowu, na onye ochi agha. O ga enye yatsy maty manota, nke ga-eme ka aghara I ma ya ikpe onwu na agbanyeghi ihe obula o mere.

N'ikpeazu mgbe Andiamihajachoro ka ha na Andriamamba dukoo ukwu n'izu ha, Ranavalona gbuoro onwe ya n'atumatu ahu.

His eyes were blue
By Ian Broinowski

'**His eyes were blue**…' I said goodnight to Nell before my shift ended and listened as she repeated it with fingers lovingly rotating her wedding ring and gazing into the corner.

There was a chair, old, patterned, comfortable and sacred to Nell.

Occasionally I suggested she wear her beautiful dress and shawl which lay dormant in her wardrobe. She would shake her head.

One evening I asked, 'Were they your husband's?'

'*No dear, not Fred's, young Charlie*'

I was stunned!

Pass me my dress dear'

I carefully laid it next to Nellie. It smelt fresh, and young and vital almost as if it had come alive after all these years. I sat on her bed, she was bright, lucid and engaged.

'*I remember a chill, then the knock. It was Charlie, propping up his bicycle with one hand and in the other…..*

Nellie paused,

…. a telegram…'

'*We were …… transfixed, held in time, it seemed like an eternity, his deep blue eyes, knowing and wanting so desperately for it to be gone. Me not wanting it, disbelieving, praying to an uncaring god, quickly he put it in my hand, our gaze broke and he was gone.*'

'*I sat in that chair, numb, not crying for days. Mum gradually coaxed me back to life, well only a half-life. 'You see. My Fred…*'

She stopped, looked at me and smiled. I waited but the moment was over, I leant forward kissed her brow and left.

Next day I went in, pulled the curtains and turned.

Nellie was in her beautiful, youthful dress, hair done and sitting in her chair. She looked so serene, a smile and unflinching eyes.

I sat for a while just to be, to stay with her as her spirit drifted away.

She was holding the telegram, the one delivered all those years ago by a boy with deep blue eyes.

I carefully took hold of the envelope and turned it over: The telegram was sealed, it had never been opened.

+++++++++++++++++++

Frederick Dougharty killed 23/4/18

Idonsashudi
Daga Ian Broinowski
Translated into Hausa by Abdulrahman.S. Waziri and Mustapha Tanko

'**ShudinIdonsa**...' Nace a kwanalafiyawa Nell kafinwa'adinaikina da saurara yadda ta ke
Jujjuyazobenauren ta a yatsar ta da kauna da kumahangendungu.
Akwaiwatatsohuwarkujera ta alfarmamaidarajaga Nell.
Lokacizuwalokacinalura ta kansakyakkyawarsuturar ta da keajiyanatsawonlokacicikin
Adakarzanami. Ta najujjuya kai.
Watayamanatambaya, 'wa 'innanmazan ki ne?'

'a-ah nawa,bandaFred,saurayi Charlie'
Nayimamaki!
'Miko mini sutuarnanawah'
A natsenaajiyedap da Nellie. Tanakamshinsabuwa da muhinmancitamkar ba tanaajiye bane nasawonshekaru ba. Na zaunaakangadonta,tayihaske,dakumadaideto.
'na tuna tsanyi, sai aka kwankwasakofa. Charlie ne, dogare da kekensa da Hanudayakumadayanna...
Nellie tayimamaki,
...tangaraho...'
'Muna...kanmu a kulle,nawanilokaci,kamarharabada,shudin. Idonsa,yabaiyanayanamutukarbukatarsa ta tafi. Ni bana so, Rashin yadda, addu'awagumaka, yayihanzariyasasu a hanuna,hashashen ta warware Kuma yatafi. Nayikwanakizauneakankujerazugum. Mama ta rarrasheninadawohayyacina, Amma b cikekkenhayyci ba. Ka gaani. Fred na...'
Ta tsaya, ta kallenitayimurmushi. Na sauraranagajeruwarlokaci,nayi
Gabanatsumbace ta goshinatafi.
Washegarinashiga,najalabulenajuya.
Nellie nasanye da kyakyawarsuturar ta zaunekankujera
Cikinkwanciyanhakali,murmushibatar da kiftaido ba.
Na zaunana dan lokaci da itahartunanin ta yagushe.
Tanarike da tangaraho,wandashekarunbayawaniyaromai

81

shudinidoyakawo.
Chikinnatsuwanakarbiambulopnajuya: tangarahonnamanne, ba a
Tababudewa ba.

FreddrickDougharty an kasha shi 23/4/18
                    "an kasha shi 23/4/18"
    Wani ba jamushe ne a lungutamkaryanasahunfarko ne a
Neteranyakarbeshi a kai
Nan ta keyamutu a safenAfirilusakanin20[th]ko 24th 1918. Bangafaruwanshi
ba.
Sa'anshi L/cpl.F.Hibberd. 7367. 12th A. I. F. B. Cc VI
wandakeFaransayanzuke tare da shi a lokaci.
    Daughartyyakasance da B. Cc. VI Pl. yazo da
24[th]Rftkumafarkonshigasasahunkenan. Gajeran
Mutum ne maiwuyansha'ani dan kimaninshekaru 30. Munakiransa Fred
mutuminHobert,
Tasmante. Mutuminkirki.
            Mai bayani L/cpl A. A. Rockliff.6620.
G. Campbell.   *12[th]Batto. A. I. C. Cc. IX*
DARTFORD.

PRESSURE POINT
By Lee Ray Khan

A low ebb here in the lobby of Hotel Odessa; tide is out, white marble bleached dry cracked....but y'know the song, *"Soooome ..times..I get a feeling.."* Oh yeah, I get a feeling all right; 'Sir, your guide is here.'
I look up. A veritable tigress of inevitability overtakes me. Whoomph. It is She. Descending a staircase (it is too much already), her narrow hips swivel w/ each kitten heeled stretch. A blonded Russian head of the old school; ice blue eyes regard me w/ an ironic glance. She. Methinks many staircases. All the better to follow, my dear. I am suddenly sassy.
She proceeds w/ a practiced, if not slightly, ever so slightly, wearied air. Another day. Another wildebeest. We are going to the usual places where we confirm something.
But now look, the piano is smashed. I understand Cubism. Her face is covered by huge Russian dark glasses. Green plastic. French 'Fully Imported' plastic, alright? Her French is fluent. And that accent. Don't start me up. Not yet anyway. Many Gauloises to be smoked. Smouldering is best.
She sits at table tossing down vodkas & holding yet another Gauloise aloft as she arches her eyebrows & laughs silently. Or she may deign to tell a story from her Russian life; She had Paris. Or it had Her. Another concert pianist. Another day. 'Oh let's run away & smuggle precious stones together, Babu.'
India, Israel, Germany, France. Oh, what a merry dance. But now. Now. Here in this Honkers hotel room. Still spinning. I look out the high window at a sea of towers. No escape. Now.
Done ring-around-the-rosie. And art & food & smoking & language & vodka & snow. Art, all that art, it's a dead give-away; who was I kidding? But here, I am now.

She, Gauloise burning between frosted lips, pours me another vodka. And another. I am lagging, behind the...er, programme. It seems. She will not be denied.

'Come! Babu!' Her accent is angular. My face, reflected everywhere is an Expressionist masterpiece [in any magazine]. As my eyes meet Hers I become The Scream.

But enough of artifice already; Her. Her body lies sunken, on a narrow cot, skeletal, her eyes glitter w/ a diamond brilliance. A small attic window admits a high pale light punctuated by the wings of pigeons. It is cold. Very cold. Ice covers the canals in the far distance. Hear it cracking? Her eyes flicker; the window. It is above her head. Her skull strains against taut white skin. 'Babu...Come.'

I rise from the spindle chair, her ice blue eyes, fixed upon the high pale light...fixed...ice blue...hear it cracking?

Nyet. She is my own. My own Russian bride. We flew across the sky (you know the one) in a donkey cart (you know the one). Some people called it art, but we, we never pulled it apart.

And now. She lays her white hand against the plate glass. Her dress is a wisp of cloud. I cannot. Her body cracks in the pale high light. I cannot. Stop it.

दबाबपोष्ट

By Lee Ray Khan
Translated into Nepelese by Lee Ray Khan

यहाँओडेसाकोलबीमाएककमईबीबी;

यसकालागिउनीहरुसँगकोसम्बन्धकोबारेमाजानकारीगराईदिनुभएकोछ। महेरिरहेछु।अनिवार्यताकोएकदमसहीबाघमलाईओभरट्याउँछ।कसम।यो त्योहो।एकसीढ़ीघटाउँदै (पहिलेनैयोधेरैनैछ), तिनकोसंकीर्णहिपहरू w / प्रत्येकबिल्लेपिरोलेघुम्न्थाल्यो।पुरानोस्कूलकोएकमुलायमरूसीटाउको; बरफनीलोआँखालेमलाई w /

एकलोभलाग्दोनजरराख्छ।त्यो।मलाईलाग्छधेरैसीढ़ीहरू।सबैभन्दारामोत पाईंपछ्याउन, मेरोप्रिय।

ईश्वरले w / कोलागीआयोजक, यदिथोपाभएन,

त्यसोभएतापनिथोरैथोपा,

वांछितवायु।अर्कोदिन।अर्कोविस्फोट।हामीसामान्यस्थानहरूमाजाँदैछौंज हाँहामीकेहिकुरापुष्टिगर्दछौं।

तरअबहेर्नुहोस्,

पियानोतोडिएकोछ।मक्यूबिजलाईबुझ्दछु।उनकोअनुहारविशालरूसीच श्मामाढाकिएकोछ।हरितप्लास्टिक।फ्रांसीसी 'पूरैआयातगरिएको' प्लास्टिक।उनकोफ्रान्सेलीधाराप्रवाहहो।

रत्योउच्चारण।मलाईसुरुनगर्नुहोस्।अझैपनिजसोछैन।धेरैग्लुलोजहरूस्मो ब्जगर्नसकिन्छ।मुस्कानउत्तमछ।

उनलेटेबलमाबस्दातलवोडाकाहरूरअझैसम्मअर्कोगौणअफ्टधारणगर्दैउनी आफ्नोआँखाबाटटाढाराख्छन्नचुपचापहल्लाउँछन्।अथवाउनीआफ्नोरूसी जीवनबाटकथाबताउनठिकहुनसक्छ;

उनीपेरिसथिए।वात्योउनकोथियो।।अर्कोसंगीतकार्यक्रमपियानोवादक।अ
र्कोदिन। 'ओहोगरौंरबाबूकोसाथमाबहुमूल्यढुङ्गाहरूगल्तीगर्छु।'
भारत, इजरायल, जर्मनी, फ्रान्स;
केएकमनननृत्य।तरअब।अहिले।यहाँयसहाईकर्सहोटलकोठामा।अझैकताई
।मटावरकोसमुद्रमाउच्चविन्डोहेर्नुहोस्।कुनैभाग्यछैन।अहिले।
रिंग-वरिपरि-रोलभयो।रकलारभोजनरधूम्रपानरभाषारवोदकारबर्फ।कला,
त्योसबैकला, योमृतदेवीहो; ममजाकगर्दैथिएँ?तरयहाँ, मअहिलेहुँ।
उनी, ग्वेलोओठकोबीचमाग्लूलोजजलाएरमलाईअर्कोवोदकाडुबाउँछन्।
रअर्को।मअफगानिस्तानमापछाडीछुट्याउँदैछु।यस्तोदेखिन्छ।त्योअस्वी
कारहुनेछैन।
'आओ!बाबू! 'उनकोउच्चारणकोणक्रमहो।मेरोअनुहार,
हरेकठाँउमाप्रतिबिम्बएक्स्पिस्टिस्टकृतिहो।मेरोआँखालेहर्सलाईभेट्छुम
स्किनबन्छु।
तरपहिलेदेखिनैशिल्पकोपर्याप्त; उनको।उनकोशरीरझन्झण्डैझण्डा,
एकसंकीर्णपुती, कंकालमा, उनकोआँखाहरुचमक /
एकहीराप्रतिभाचमक।एकसानोअटारीविन्डोकबूतरकोपंखोंद्वारापतितउ
च्चपीलाप्रकाशकोस्वीकारगर्दछ।योचिसोछ।धेरैचिसो।बर्फलामोदूरीमानह
रहरू।योकुकुरसुन्नुहोस्?
उनकोआँखाझन्झटइयाल।योउनकोटाउकोमाथिछ।उनकोखोपड़ीकोटसेतो
छालाकोविरूद्धस्ट्रिअन। 'बाबू … आउनुहोस्।'
मस्पिन्डकुर्सीबाटउठेको, उनकोआउँनिलोआँखा, उच्चपहेंलोप्रकाशमातय
… तय … बर्फनीलो … योघुमाउनसुन्न?
Nyet।त्योमेरोहो।मेरोआफ्नैरूसीदुलही।हामीगधाकोकार्टमा
(तपाईंलाईथाहाछ) आकाशमाउड्यौं

86

(तपाइँलाईथाहाछ)।केहीमानिसहरूलेयसलाईकलाभनिन्, तरहामी,
हामीलेयसलाईकहिल्यैबिर्सनसकेनौ।

रअब।उनलेप्लेटगिलासविरुद्धआफ्नोसेतोहातलिन्छिन्।उनकोपोशाकक्ला
उडकोबुद्धिमानीहो।मसक्किदन।उनकोशरीरपीलाउच्चप्रकाशमादरार।मस
क्किदन।बन्दगर।

ooOoo

Reminiscences

By Mona Lisa Jena

…..″I am past 100 years and six months in age now. There is no one of my time alive any more... I have done so much for so many…. The rickshawalla didn't take any fare from me, said, 'Go mother! How can I take money from you?' I had gone to Ananda Bazaar; it will be past three in the afternoon when they will eat lunch. I could not wait that long. So, I came away. Just because you will feed me something for lunch, should I travel such a long distance everyday! Whatever is there with you, do serve me, my daughter...″Kaia bou, the mother of Kaia, went on mumbling…

It was already noon, and in summer the heat was at its peak in the month of June. Sujata fasts on Mondays. Her son and husband were out of town, she did not cook … luckily, and someone had sent vegetarian cooked offerings from the temple. She was yet to eat when the old woman came. She knew the old woman was fond of fish, "Aunty, I cannot give you fish today. Will you eat the temple offerings?" The old woman was very hungry and she sat down to eat. Sujata put the food on a plantain leaf on the floor. She added some vegetable curry that she had, and a tumbler with drinking water... she also kept a jug of water for the woman to wash herself. While the old woman was eating, Sujata got busy with her household chores. On a holiday, her chores multiply, she could not afford to sit by the woman and keep talking. Besides, the old woman would say the same things over and over again.

Actually she was thinking about Kaiabou, the old woman, for some time. She was contemplating sending her some food and a quilt as winter was near, but she was busy and could not find time. That day, when Kaiabou came along, she at least could afford to serve her something to eat.

When the old woman got up to dump the used plantain leaf plate outside, Sujata rushed to stop her as it is not proper to allow old people to lift their own plates. But Kaiabou refused to let her do so, saying, "You have served me food. Now, how can you pick up my dirty leaf plate?"

When she was refusing to let Sujata pick up her plate, Sujata was already out in the front yard of the house. Outside someone's cow was grazing; she would gobble up everything, including the soiled banana leaf. Kaiabou blessed her saying, "May the auspicious bangles on your hands and the vermillion mark in the parting of your head remain forever, May God bless you...."

After that, she came and sat on a high stool. She had trouble in sitting on the floor. It was more difficult for her to get up from the floor. It is tough too to lift a tall woman of five feet –seven- inches... But she was tottering all over the village, holding on to an antique walking stick...Kaiabou could no longer walk straight. She was bent from her waist.

Kaiabou was a tall and stout woman in her heyday. Even at 100, her eyes are sharp and piercing, her face retained those sharp contours. Although her cheeks are now hollowed, the bones give her face the character of a competent woman. She was not at all fragile; like the Barunai hill and the centuries-old banyan trees abounding in the forests of the hill, Kaiabou's wrinkles were strong and meaningful.

People in a village always pay special attention to a person who lives up to 100 years. They are treated with respect, they would talk about many secrets of the families, of the trees, they would predict the rains when the clouds touched the peak of the Barunai Hills, and whether there will be a bountiful crop or not. Many people liked to obtain her blessings when they got married, and when they had children they would bring them to seek her blessings and gave her money and food.

...."I have seen so many people dying before my eyes. But I wonder why I am not dying?" Kaiabou continued. She kept on muttering to herself... "Not very long. This season, I will be gone. Guna's wife says if I die before Kana's death anniversary this year, she would get her son married. She is waiting for my death. She curses me for not dying soon. What can I do? It is still eight months for Kana's death anniversary...I will certainly be gone. Definitely... no one in my family died ailing from any illness for long... everybody died suddenly, without suffering. ... Guna's wife was mixing poison in my food. But that could not kill me.... I am surviving. I had good food when I was a child. That is why I keep well and live so long.... ." she sighed.

...."My father was an expert huntsman. He was tall, well built, almost like a giant to look at. He had long hair all over his body. We nicknamed him 'chimpanzee', wild man. He had two wives. From both of them there were 18 children. I am the eldest. Only two of my stepbrothers are alive today. They have also grown old... I cannot go to meet them now. Who will take me there? Kaia and Baia, my two sons are tossing me around like an unwanted sack. My brothers are also not in a condition to come this side to see me. After my father died, what is there left in your parental home?"...she kept quiet for a few minutes staring at Sujata, who was busy like a whirlwind.

"He used to hunt spotted deer, sambar and barking deer from the jungles at Barunai hills. We were eating one kilo of meat along with one sera (about 50 tolas) rice. My father was so stout and well built that we could not hold his arms or legs in our palms. We could not massage him. That is why he had prepared a wooden plank and kept that polished and smeared with mustard oil. We could thump it on his body to relieve his muscle pain... that time, one Sera of rice cost seven paisa and one kilo mutton cost 35 paisa..."

That day, Kaiabou was in a great mood. The stories were not new for Sujata. Sadness filled her heart when she would listen to the narrative. Kaiabou had taken care of her three children when they were infants; she would clean their excreta, bathe them after rubbing them with turmeric paste which she would herself grind into a smooth paste. She would rub the Rasi oil with her strong hands to make their tender bones strong.

Kaiabou continued, she was not bothered whether there was any listener for her story or not...

....." When I was only 15, my father had married me off in Gangapda village... I had taken with me ornaments like *Bauti* (armlet), *Pahuda* (payal), *Chandrahara* (necklace shaped like a moon), *Bichhahara* (necklace shaped like a scorpion with interwoven rings) and lots of gold and silver coins worth fifty kilos as my dowry. Barely a year after my marriage, my husband left for Rangoon. Immediately after that World War II started. He didn't come back for the next four/five years. He did not look after his aged parents. There was no news from him either. There was no one to give us any information about him, whether he was dead or alive. And here he was the only son of my in-laws. He was a mason by profession. That year, as there was no one to look after the rice field, no cultivation was done. Drought affected us very badly. My husband had gone to work as a mason at Rangoon. He had gone by ship. I took upon myself the entire responsibilities. I looked after my in-laws. Cooked and fed and served them in earnest. I have served them so well. I was very sincere. Everyone in the village would swear by this."

....Then one day, my husband came back. He had brought another woman with him, a Burmese woman. She had brought with her lots of gold. I have noticed. My husband had dug a hole in the floor and had hidden them there. My in laws died shortly afterwards. I could not stay there for long. So I came to my parental home. When I left I brought with me all the gold ornaments that I took during my wedding...."

Kaiabou's face would become very tense even years after, when she would narrate the episode. Sujata sat on the cot nearby. She felt sad for her. Should she cook her own meal at this advanced age and clean her own soiled clothes! Her son and his wife would not make a bed for her even

Sujata asked, "Those days many people had two wives. Why did you leave your husband and your home?"

When she is reminded of those hurtful days, Kaiabou's heart writhes in pain. The one she would be waiting for years together, would return after five years and with a new wife? This Burmese woman was completely different from Kaliabou. She had a wheatish complexion, long pitch black hair. Her hair was so long that it would sweep the floor if left undone. Her smiling face looked like that of a 12/13-year-old girl: completely devoid of any resentment or hatred. When was her face visible? She would plaster her face with a sandalwood paste. Her attire was also very peculiar. She remained inside the house keeping it sparkling clean. Being a foreigner so untouchable , she was not allowed inside the kitchen. . Kaiabou, then called Suli, was in charge. Unlike her, Suli was capable of handling her hearth and the vast landed property that they owned.

Suli's Rangoon- returned husband told her, "You also stay here as my wife. She is like your younger sister. You will look after the outside work. And she will take care of the home..."

But when Suli heard this, her anger knew no bounds. She had looked after the entire household alone till now. Just because she could not bear a child even after four five years of marriage, she was ridiculed for being a barren woman by the neighbors. And yet this Burmese woman came and she came with a child in her womb? Was she anybody's maid in waiting? That is why she left her husband's house in a huff for good. She took those gold and silver ornaments that her father had given in dowry. But the Burmese woman was really pretty. While Suli was very tall, the Burmese woman was petite, blessed with shining long hair. She was very quiet, very docile. After ages also, Suli can commit to memory her charming face with tenderness.

Suli nee Kaiabou always talked about these things, she would talk agitatedly, with many twists, and it seems like a story, not her real life. Usually old people tell us stories, stories about the rustic village folks, about the prince and his adventures about 'Chakulia Panda', the wandering Brahmin. Sujata too had a turmeric paste and mustard oil massage by this woman when she was an infant. She has been listening to the same tales from Kaiabou for the last forty years. Her mother would treat the old woman nicely; Kaiabou would take tea with breakfast at their home and Sujata's mother would continue her chores while keeping an ear on Kaiabou's rattling.

When years later Sujata became a mother, Kaiabou was sought for. And once more the same narrative was repeated. Nothing was made-up. Sujata would think, even if people speak unkindly about this woman because of her haughty character, how independent she was in her spirits! She envied her co-wife so much that she decided to leave her husband and her marital home! She was illiterate, but Kaiabou was terrific at accounting. She was like a virtual walking tehsil office with her ready information about the details of money matters, ornaments, land records....

Once again Kaiabou continued her story... "I was married off at the age of fifteen, and then I came back to stay at my father's home for another 12 years. At that time, my father again married me off in this village. My second husband's first wife was a quarrelsome woman. I bore my husband three children. When they were born, I would ask for their grandmother to look after them. She would come and after I delivered, she would go back. Those days, we were not allowed to stay in our house during childbirth. We would shift to a makeshift cottage at the edge of our village. Then after delivering a child we would continue to stay there for another week or ten days. Only then we could come back to our home with the child.

.... Out of many children that my parents had, only I survived. That is why after my mother died in childbirth, my father brought home a very young girl and kept her. She was even younger to me. I dug up my jewellery from that house and brought it with me. From that day, I could not get along with my father. We owned 180 (9 Bati) acres of landed property. Almost half of the paddy field here actually belongs to us…

…the jewellery I had brought with me then, helped in constructing the concrete house I live in now. One room cost ten rupees those days to build. But that Mahura, the mason, was a swindler. The house is in a semi-dilapidated condition now. How bad is his workmanship?"

Sujata knows about these things. In the very house, this old woman does not have a space to call her own now. She would sleep curling up in the open; otherwise she would sleep in the narrow mud plastered front yard of the house. It would be inadequate for a tall woman like her. She cannot stand straight; would stoop when she walked. But seeing her constitution, one can easily guess how well built she must have been during her younger days. Sujata had once reprimanded her son Kaia, saying, "Your mother has struggled so much to raise you all. Despite having so much, how hopeless you sons are now! Will you keep neglecting her in her old age?"…. After that, Kaiabou got to sleep in the verandah of their concrete house.

…" the elder daughter in law took away all the ornaments and the large brass utensils as well. When she got her eldest daughter married, she gave everything to her… they are not giving me enough to eat now. I get the government pension of three hundred rupees quite late, after 15th day of the month… when Kumara's son comes he would stop his vehicle and put a hundred rupee note in my hand. He had, after a gap of five months, come and given me five hundred rupees. That is all. He has not come since then. Birakishore's son was asking about me at the market place, "how is the old woman…?" Kaia told him, The old woman has died since long…..

… Just because I had brought so much of wealth with me, you are able to make a decent living now. That house was built by me only. Hema, my daughter, is also facing a hard life in her in-law's place in Bhubaneswar. She is suffering badly. She told me, "It is ironic that Bou (mother), neither you are dying, nor I am dying. You don't even get a handful to eat, your clothes smell so filthy, and you cannot even wash them well..."

It is true that Kaiabou always liked to live with dignity. Her clothes were always very clean, she never smelled foul in her life. Now when her daughter visited her occasionally, she would boil a bucketful of water and put her mother's dirty clothes in detergent for some time and wash them clean. But of late, even she was facing difficulty to come. She too is past 70 years in age.

.... "At Ananda Bazaar, it was different when Hari Sahu's wife was alive. That time I used to go regularly to eat my meal there. When it would be harvesting time, I would prepare cakes like *Monda* and *enduri* for the family. After her death, the family eats at three in the afternoon. They are very lazy. There is a woman to help in the household chores. She would come in the morning and sweep and clean the house. By the time the women of the family wake up it is past nine in the morning. The youngest son is not married yet. The only daughter never came after her marriage. When she was married, she was too skinny. She did not have a fleck of flesh on her skeleton like body.... Her eyes were big and would bulge out. She was 45 then. No one chose the girl for a bride. In the end they had married her off in Jatni, but the groom was very handsome to look at. How desperate was Hari Sahu before his son in law! He gave him a two-storey building right in the centre of the bazaar complex in Jatni along with plenty of landed property as dowry. He gave him all the gold ornaments that he had kept from Balia's booty. But after that I have never got to see that girl. If there is any death ceremony or other ceremonies, only the son-in-law came and went back before sunset... What will happen with all this property? Before my own eyes, their wealth multiplied! But did anything remain? You will see, everything will be gone from them...This generation is enjoying that property now! In the entire Khurda zone, half the landed property belonged to the Hari Sahu family. And half of this locality also belonged to my family. My youngest son sold a large chunk of my land to the Pattanayak family at throwaway price! In official records, the land still belongs to us. On Patta (paper), it belongs to my father in law. Recently, my son sold it for Rupees 40 thousand only, he did not give me a single paisa out of the sale... they are selling paddy now, and not taking the pain to get rice out of it. My younger son sold the half boiled paddy at 20 rupees per kilo... he never seeks my permission, never consults me for anything. They don't give me food to eat.

... What do I need? A little of fish or mutton will do. My daughters in law don't cook non-vegetarian food at home now. They say the house will smell foul. But I don't have the appetite for bland food. I am used to good food since my childhood. Now, how can I swallow the food if it has no taste? Shall I travel all the way everyday to eat my meal? Till they were alive, it was a different issue. What did I not do for them? I took the entire responsibility of their household. Their keys were with me. I knew every detail about their household and where they stored what was known to me. One day they could not find a two-seer weight worth gold chain. They were not able to find it after three/four days' desperate searching. At last I was called for. I went and found the ornament and gave to them..."

.... They had dug up the floor inside their home and built iron safes below. They had stored all the booty that they received from Balia there. Balia, the farmer, was a notorious dacoit those days. He would roam the dense forests of Ranpur hills unbridled. He had three or four wives. But he would help the needy people everywhere whenever he came across them. That is why he was very popular among the poor. He would reach Hari Sahu's home at past midnight. Hari Sahu himself would serve him food on a Sal leaf plate. Servants were not allowed to come nearby. Balia, the farmer who would be completely drunk at that time, would pour all the gold, silver jewellery that he would have burgled wrapped in a *gamochha,* on the mattress there. Hari Sahu would pick them up and keep them in a safe place. Then he would pick up Balia's soiled plate and clean the place. No one would come there; no one would help Hari Sahu as well. With the loot, Hari Sahu became so rich afterwards. But could Hari Sahu manage all that wealth! His children went astray. They are enjoying that wealth even now. They are managing by selling their land. The youngest son is now past forty. He is not married. He is slightly mad. They have only one daughter. After she was married off, she has never stepped into her parental home...

The ornaments and gold coins that were stored in the underground iron safe were destroyed when water from the rice field seeped into it.....''

Sometimes, Kaiabou talks like this, as if her eyes can foresee something untoward happening. As if she could see those days clearly as a film! Can anyone say that such a strong woman can ever shed tears? She was a tough woman. A very strong woman... she would say, will such wealth and properties last forever? There would be no water in the pond, there would not be any fish in the stream, and there would be no crop in the field.....

Kaiabou continued, "I have given food to so many daughters and daughters-in-law. I have saved many lives from being ruined. Even now when Sadhu's daughter in law sees me she would clutch my hands and weep. When my daughter Hema was born, my mother in law was not alive, otherwise seeing a daughter she would have remarked sarcastically, it is a snail only! She suffered very badly in her old age. My younger sister in law neglected her. But my mother-in-law also had tormented her a lot!... she was such a miser that she would distribute one seer rice among five person while a sack full of rice would be rotting in the store... whenever anybody delivered in your village, I was the most sought after. I would massage the infants properly with turmeric paste and oil. If there would be a daughter, the mother-in-law would not give them anything to eat... those days I was the midwife delivering the child. For my delivery, my grandmother used to come to help. Those days there used to be a doctor in our locality and he used to stay at Anand Bazaar. ... I have never seen any Gora sahib. I have no memory about the days when our country became independent too.... But who was visiting a doctor those days?

Those days mothers-in-law were very hard hearted. A newlywed bride would always remain in perpetual fear of her. If she gave birth to a daughter, her mother-in-law will not give her rice till eleven in the morning. And the young woman would be lying on her makeshift bed like a dying woman after childbirth. I would send piping hot rice mixed with cloves, ghee, and black cumin seeds wrapped in a Sal leaf and then tied with paddy sheaf so that their mother-in-law will not be able to know. Many a time we would carry hot food hidden in a cloth wrap. I have saved so many lives like this! That is why I am fed by so many people today."

Sujata interrupted her asking, "what happened to that Balia, the farmer?"

Kaiabou smiled when she reminisced about those days. She said, "The police could never catch Balia dacoit then. One day one of his assistants betrayed him for money and informed the police about his whereabouts. But could Balia dacoit be trapped even then! He knew some black magic. That is how he could accomplish his thefts so smoothly. He was not afraid of anyone. Nobody would give any information about him. Everybody benefited from him. If someone needed money for a wedding, they would send word to Balia, the dacoit. He would fetch lots of wealth and keep it at the house. He was very helpful as a human being. He would be wearing lots of rings to appease unhappy planets and the gods...."

Sujata said, "You will live at least till my daughter's marriage. You will bless her. Don't feel hurt about your children. What can we do? He is your son after all! Why did he stop his canteen business? It was running well! What will you do with money at this age? Let them live in happiness. Your sweetmeat shop was the biggest in town; if it could be there now, I would not have to worry for my daughter's wedding... you have taken so much care of my children...!"

Kaiabou was calm.

She said, "They are saying I am being haunted by a spirit. Eighteen of my father's children did not survive. He would kill them at childbirth itself. They are saying that the spirit haunts me too. He would drag me from one place and dump me at another. That is why they are putting a big lock at the gate so that the spirit cannot drag me away..."

Sujata said, "My mother-in-law's death anniversary is next Saturday. I will not go to my in-law's place. I will do the ceremony here only, invite the priest and give him vegetables and rice. You come that day. You knew her well. She is gone since two years..."

Kaiabou blurted midway. She said sarcastically, "Ah yes, yes I remember...how she used to torment you! I have seen them all. Have I not seen? She would always behave in a wicked way, to such a nice girl like you. Son will be sleeping; his mother will also be sleeping; only you slogged all the time. You were winnowing a sack full of rice even when you were carrying your child. Your mother-in-law was not a good woman, my dear! You will never have any problem. God is watching everything. You will always get to wear your auspicious bangles and vermillion mark on your head and live happily with your husband and family. No one will be turned away from your door. No one will leave without eating from your hands. Your kitchen will never fall short. My blessings are with you. I will certainly come. Do give me a sweater before winter. My belongings are not in place. I am getting careless and people are stealing my goods ..."

Kaiabou was at the *Dasadol melana* field on the last day of the five-day-long festival after Holi... she was fuming. As if her two big eyes were spitting fire that evening. She was grumbling angrily, "Baia, my youngest son and his daughter have thrown me out the home! They have driven me away. Kaia, my son had drowned in this temple pond. Tonight I will also die in this pond." Her rage was something to watch that evening. She refused flatly to go back. Everybody sat in a ring around her to prevent her from jumping into the pond. Policemen also gave protection so that such untoward incident does not take place. Throughout the night four strong built young men guarded the old women.

In the early morning she had come to Sujata's door and was knocking noisily. Everyone got up. They made her sit and tried to soothe her frayed nerves. Sujata served her left over mutton curry with rice.

Kaiabou was constantly saying, "Nothing will happen to me. My father had fed me well. He would put animal blood in the hollow of a bamboo, burn it in the fire and then give it to me to eat. I can digest everything even at this age,"

Sujata's son was at home that time. Kaiabou asked him, "Leave me at my home on your scooter now. Don't worry, I will not fall..."

Lo and behold, the old woman sat behind Sujata's son confidently, at the age of 100 years! She didn't shake at all, said Sujata's son when he returned. Kaiabou's family is really very cruel, he lamented, "they are shameless, mother! They are starving her. She has no place to call her own there and on my face they are asking why the old woman is not dying!"

It was translucent as oral history. And those old people were rock-solid and profound. They were different and they carried with them the entire burden of a tradition. They are like very old trees, with their roots buried deep, in the depths of tradition. They live according to their own dictum, and express themselves according to their own will. They have seen so much of turbulent lives, suffered so much pain, humiliation, neglect and their near and dear one's numerous deaths, and yet how they keep alive their human souls, with so much of enthusiasm, happiness! Within those hundred year-old bones such longings for love and attachment, and their cravings to bless their young ones all the time...! As if one chapter of live history was walking away! No, not only history, she was like a legend herself beyond the pages of history.

SCARLET
By Ayo Oyeku

The wind blew in rasps. The young woman snatched at her wrapper, mindful of it from being blown away. But the little child strapped on her back, snored through the cold night. While the older ones, dozed on their tired legs.

She knocked softly on an old wooden door. The sound echoed into the dead of the night; reverberating against the walls of the village huts. The young woman shuddered with fear. She glanced here and there; to be sure no villager was awakening by her knocks.

The old wooden door creaked open. And an emaciated old woman appeared at the front door. A senescent languor was stealing over the old woman's time. The lamp in her hand shook. A huge surprise lit on the face of the old woman. The two women stared blankly at each other, as an uncertain strangeness began to feed on their consciousness.

The young woman's lips quivered under a weight of guilt. It's been seven years since she visited her mother-in-law. She wondered if her mother-in-law could ever forgive her. Now that an irreparable enigma had brought them together again; she knew her chances were slim. Fresh tears brewed over her guilty eyes.

"Come," the old woman said.

The young woman hurried towards her. The old woman caught her in a deep embrace. The young woman began to sob uncontrollably. She slipped downwards to her mother-in-law's knees, clinging to the old woman's right leg; pleading.

"Stop crying Lade, let's go inside."

Lade stopped crying, and sniffled to hold back the tears. She let go of her mother-in-laws leg. The old woman led the way into the dark and stuffy hut. And Lade followed meekly with her children.

The old woman looked for a proper position to place the lamp, while Lade stared around the hut. The old hut hadn't changed much.

The rough clay walls now paved with crannies. Ancestral shadows now found sentinel within the nooks of the hut. Two wooden stools were flung at different corners. Two mats were also rolled up against the wall, while other edifying objects hung at different positions within the small hut. The air in the room was fragrant with scents coming from Garden Basil leaves collected in a small pot.

The old woman reappeared from one of the rooms in the hut, holding a large bowl of water and a clean piece of cloth.

"It must have been a long journey." The old woman spoke warmly, knowing they must have travelled by lorry down to the village. Lade watched as her mother-in-law soaked the cloth, squeezed it and applied it on the head and arms of her grandchildren. She offered to assist, but the old woman refused.

"I should have bathed them. But I don't want to wake my neighbours." She added, and Lade could not help but admire her mother-in-law's love, care and unfailing kindness. They had once shared this cosy relationship, until the city took her and her husband away from the village. Lade smiled with the corner of her mouth as she watched her mother-in-law touch her grandchildren with rectitude of motherhood. Lade left to empty the bowl of water, before she returned, her mother-in-law had spread the mats on the floor. Lade laid her children on a mat, and slept beside them.

"Lade, you are my daughter. We must share a mat."

Her mother-in-law's utterance sent a cold chill down her spine. She rose up quietly and joined her mother-in-law on the other mat. The old woman did not say a word again, rather, she took the lamp from where it stood, and blew it off.

A thick blanket of darkness enveloped the whole room. The room became silent. Lade changed sleeping positions. She could hardly sleep. Fresh thoughts of her doting husband's demise began to brood over her. He had always been an active and vivacious, broad-chest man. He earned a good living as a resourceful business tycoon. He was often away on business trips, but whenever he was around, he showered abundance of love and care on his family. He treated them with delight and they all relished his absence.

A strange illness took over him. He began to emaciate, and at a point, he began to lose taste for food. The high-spiritedness in him was sapped away by the parasitic illness. The doctor had diagnosed him for tuberculosis. But he had argued it was a spiritual attack from his unknown enemies. He refused to go for treatment, as his case worsened. A marshmallow of sensations took over Lade, as her once enviably handsome husband now had his face pockmarked by pox, and swellings hung on different portions of his skin.

A garb of trepidation enclosed Lade. She fought for her dear husband's life, as a convict would struggle with a hangman's noose. Her children were deprived of the attention and care she once offered generously. She had equally lost the beauty of her motherhood under the weight of stress and tears.

At night, he began apologising. He begged her without a vivid reason. His voice was wrapped in agony and pains. Lade never understood. She begged him to be silent, because he had not offended her in any way. This truth hung on the leaden conscience of their wedlock. But she misunderstood it for his throes of death. Because that night; he became a flood of rain without refuge.

Hot tears bubbled to the surface of her eyes. A tear escaped, and rolled sideways. More tears followed, rolling downwards her ear-lobes. The frail mat absorbed her tears without remorse. Lade sniffled.

"The priceless pot had been shattered. We must take heart."

The words echoed within the dark hut. It had come from the lips of a mother, who had lost her only child. Lade's heartbeat ceased for a few seconds. She had heard her mother-in-law's voice. The old woman was not asleep. A tear clung to her throat. She sniffled and pushed it down her lungs.

The old woman now sat up, and spoke "Won't my enemies make mockery of me when they watch my large mouth with tears?" She sighed and continued, "He was my only child." Suddenly, the old woman burst into loud tears saying "a curse be on the day he was born! Perhaps if he had not been born, I would not have experienced this endless heartache at old age!"

Lade became ashamed of herself. She was supposed to harness the old woman's fortitude. But she had brought back the memories that were meant to be shared in their solitude. She hurriedly moved closer to her mother-in-law, and held her in a deep embrace.

"Look," the old woman spoke in a garbled manner, pointing to the children who were sound asleep, "those are our tiny acorns, they will grow into a large oak – comforting us with their shades during sunny times, bringing back our halcyon days." Lade marvelled at her mother-in-law's wisdom. Truly, the children were their hope. Lade apologised to her mother-in-law, and they both lay on their backs, and slept.

The first morning sunlight found the two women at the backyard of the hut. Lade busied bathing her children, while her mother-in-law prepared their breakfast at the cooking shed.

"I never knew you now have a baby girl?" The mother-in-law cuts in.

"Yes, I do, mama. Utah is 7 months old."

Lade could still remember how she and her husband had travelled to the village in celebration of the birth of their first child. It was 7 years back. The good news of their second child's birth, two years after, was only sent to her mother-in-law in the village. Lade now narrated to her mother-in-law, how Utah had been born a few months before her husband's sudden illness and eventual demise.

"What does Utah mean?" The old woman inquired.

"Actually my husband had named our daughter after one of the American states he visited years back." She replied softly.

Lade could hear her mother-in-law make a jocularly remark about them treading upon the African culture and ethics, for Western civilisation, and they burst into a hearty peel of laughter. Lade's

105

mother-in-law also shared corny anecdotes about her son's childhood bathing experiences, and they all laughed hilariously.

Her mother-in-law was still cooking when she led her freshly bathed children back into the hut. Her emergence into the hut was halted by two elderly women, who were already waiting. She was slightly shocked. The two women gave a ghostly stare at her. Lade recognised their faces and she hurriedly knelt down before them, greeting. But they ignored her.

A sullen atmosphere charged the small hut. The elderly women moved from side to side, with their arms crossed behind their backs, staring at Lade and her children with a grave look. They hissed and sighed. Lade trembled on her knees. She fidgeted at the edge of her wrapper. The electrifying silence did not last long, when one of the women bellowed,

"You are a witch!"

"Now that you have killed our son, what have you come to do? Do you want to kill our friend too?" The second woman hollered too.

"Vampire, you cannot suck our friend's blood; neither can you kill her grandchildren! We shall take them from you, and fling you out of our village!" The two women chorused discordantly.

Lade could not hold back her feelings. She burst into loud tears.

"Stop shedding crocodile tears. You are a witch!!" The two women chorused again. They hissed and muttered disgusting words at Lade.

"Keep quiet women! How can you utter such disgusting things?" The two women were taken aback by their friend's sudden appearance and sharp response. Lade's mother-in-law had heard some noise coming from her hut and had rushed in to see what it was. And she was totally displeased by her friends' reactions towards her daughter-in-law.

"Have you been bewitched?" One of the elderly women forced a reply from her wonder-struck mouth.

In response, Lade's mother-in-law hurried to the corner of her hut and grabbed a broom. "Get out!" She screamed, and wielded the broom at her friends. The startled elderly women retraced their steps and hurried out of the hut. After they had left, the old woman helped her daughter-in-law back to her feet and also encouraged her to always stand up for the truth. Lade felt totally indebted to her mother-in-law.

The subsequent days in the village had turned out very peaceful for Lade, her children, and her mother-in-law. Except for Utah; who had developed a sudden fever. The little child suffered a high temperature at night, and she was often restless. Lade knew she had to visit the hospital.

The path to the village hospital turned out as Lade's mother-in-law had described. Otiose bushes flanked both sides of the clay road. The winding path unfurled at the end, opening in-between two huge hills. The small, but beautiful village hospital stood afar off, as a perfect grandeur for the mitigating landscape.

"We would carry out some blood tests on your daughter..." the doctor, a pleasant man in his early middle age retorts, after listening to Lade's observations on her little child. After taking Utah's blood sample, the doctor gave Lade some drugs to alleviate the little girl's pain, and told Lade to come back in a week's time for the blood test result. Lade left the hospital, relieved.

Nights after the hospital visit, Utah's health grew worse. The clouds began to scurry away from the sky. And the sullen sky began to ignite with silent lightening. The children panicked under the sound of an unexpected thunderstorm, but Lade's panic was worse. Utah was convulsing!

"Mama, what shall I do?"

Lade expressed herself in a garbled manner. A miasma of trepidation swept over her as she watched her helpless child throw fits within the small hut. The older children cried as they watched the restlessness of their little sister. The nervous mother-in-law disappeared into one of the rooms and reappeared with a bottle of palm-oil. Lade carefully held her daughter's head firmly and allowed her mother-in-law scoop some palm-oil in the girl's mouth.

"That should alleviate it."

Lade's mother-in-law blurted out from her weary lungs. After a short while, the traditional therapy helped subside the violent movements of the little child. A deep thunderstorm struck, and a huge torrent of rain followed. Utah had become calm, but her skin was pale, and her pupils were rolled inwards.

"I have to take her to the hospital!"

Lade exclaimed. There was a short silence. Lade knew her mother-in-law was considering the weather condition; it was raining heavily, and the journey down to the village hospital at night was worth discouraging. Lade watched her mother-in-law dash into the room to bring out a thick woollen wrapper. The two women knew they had to do everything possible to salvage the little girl's life. Lade hurriedly strapped her daughter to her back, and her mother-in-law ensured the wrapper protected the child from being drenched by the rain. The old woman offered to follow her, but Lade persuaded her to stay with the other children.

Lade dashed into the rain. The rain showered down as piercing arrows, and caught the helpless mother in a blind sway. Rivulets of rain seeped through her hairs, spread out; some rushing down her eyelids, others around her ears and face, all collected at the trunk of her neck; running downwards through her cleavage. Her cloth was soaked. She perpetually wiped her eyes, in order to see the road clearly, as she ran through the night.

As she took the final winding through the hills, she missed her steps and slipped. The muddy soil swept her off her feet, and she landed on the soil with the back of her hands. Quickly, she swiped at the muddy path and sprang back to her feet. She hurried downwards into the hospital, oblivious of the muddy stains around her cloth, hands and calves.

Lade was met with an emergency reception from the hospital nurses. Utah was wheeled into a ward, and Lade was made to wait at the reception. She panted and prayed silently for her dear child.

Lade's mother-in-law wandered around the hut. A stultifying atmosphere enveloped her thoughts. She wondered what was now happening to her daughter-in-law and her granddaughter. Her frail heart wasn't at rest. Neither could she sleep. Seeing that the two older children were now sound asleep; she locked them in the hut, and dashed into the heavy rain.

Lade seemed to gurgle out from a nightmarish maze. She found herself now being surrounded by the preying eyes of the nurses. They helped her to her feet. Lade wondered what had happened to her in the past few minutes. Seeing that she was now fully conscious, the nurses helped her into the doctor's office. Sitting straight up, she stared into the gentle eyes of the doctor.

"Am sorry, Madam."

The doctor's plea made her body tremble. Her mind triggered backwards. She could remember she had collapsed when the doctor informed her about the death of her little child. She sighed deeply, but remained calm.

"Can I see your husband?"

The doctor's question sent a cold chill down her spine. Bitter memories flushed her sublime beauty away. A hot tear escaped from the confluence of tears above her eyes. She muttered something negative. And the doctor understood her husband was late. Lade clenched her teeth, to hold back the tears when the doctor apologised again. She observed that the doctor became hesitant about what he then wanted to say, but she urged him to. The words slurred out from the doctor's lips.

"The result of the blood test showed that your daughter's death is an aftermath of the HIV/AIDS disease."

Lade's breath ceased. She had felt a sudden pang in her heart. She found herself rooted to her seat. She felt no tear. She just stared into oblivion. A fleeting glimpse of indecipherable memories flashed before her eyes. She then understood why her husband was reluctant to make love to her in the past months. She also understood why he refused to be taken to the hospital in his dying moments. She could then understand his pleas at the brink of death. She understood...everything.

Lade smiled. The doctor smiled back. Pleased by the way she comported herself, he went on explaining how she could possibly live a healthy life with the disease. The doctor's words flew past her ears. Suddenly she burst into wild tears. She sobbed, lamented and even cursed herself. The doctor's comforting words could not assuage her feelings.

Suddenly she stopped crying. She quickly wiped her tears with the edge of her wrapper. Lade had heard her mother-in-law's voice at the reception. The poor old woman did not deserve to share in this agony. The old woman believed her grandchildren would definitely become great oaks that would comfort them during sunny days. Lade knew she had lost a tiny acorn that night, but she definitely had two acorns in the hut that would become great oaks. If this dream were to come true, she must be ready to weather the storms ahead.

She sprang up and walked out of the doctor's office. The doctor was caught in a web of surprises. He was speechless. He sprang up too, and followed her quickly. Lade met her mother-in-law still making inquiry about her and her granddaughter from the nurses, who were unwilling to give her any response. She caught the depression in her mother-in-laws eyes, but brushed it off with a sigh. She simply walked towards her, smiling.

"Come, Mama. We must return home."

The old woman succumbed gently. She laid her hand into Lade's own and they both walked back into the night. The rain now drizzled silently. The two women walked home without saying a word to each other. The old woman knew they were returning home without the child. But she did not understand everything.

Poetry

人生之水
By Changming Yuan

山泉清甜
晨露晶莹

而淌过心脏的流体
必须像海水一样浩淼
混浊如泪
苦咸如汗

Water of Life
By Changming Yuan
Translated from Chinese by Changming Yuan

sweet is
the spring water, and
crystal-clear
are the mountain dews

but flowing through our hearts
is a fluid
as salty as seawater
like sweat, like tears

思想猎人

By Changming Yuan

我遁着它的身后
偷偷潜入茂密的森林
突然，它消失得无影无踪
不知它是否还会折返

久久静伏在幽深处
我渐渐似有所悟：
丛林中本无猎物
只有追寻

Thought Hunting
By Changming Yuan
Translated from Chinese by Changming Yuan

stalking behind it
i sneaked into the thick forest
where it suddenly vanished
i did not know when, even whether
it would reappear at all

lying long in ambush
at the heart of silences
i became increasingly aware
the jungle has no prey in the first place
except hunting per se

追求

By Changming Yuan

在一半是黑暗的世界
你的身体在恶梦中
浸泡，腐烂

而你的心
可像同步卫星那样
在高空漫游
把长夜远远甩在身后

只要你的心飞的够高够快
你会永享光明

Pursuing
By Changming Yuan
Translated from Chinese by Changming Yuan

in a world half in darkness
your body is soaked in a nightmare
rotting

but your heart
can roam like a synchronous satellite
in a high altitude, leaving
the long night far behind

as long as your heart flies fast and high enough
you will enjoy light forever

图腾柱
诗 / 陶志健

站在故土的荒草中，泥沼边
身躯已经断掉了大半
你在守望着什么
像一位老人
风烛残年
这里已经没有了勇敢的猎手
没有女人孩子盼望他带回美餐；
没有人再需要你的护佑
没有人再需要你——
把他的故事记录
把他的心智充满
这里也没有了一座座帐篷
烘托你的辉煌和高大
把你作为他们的史迹
他们生生不息的标杆——
没有它们站立在
你的周围
为你做伴
可，为什么你没有去
像你的兄弟一样
到那旖旎而熙攘的公园
去点缀整洁美丽的景致？
那里能吸引众多的目光
能进入无数的照片
给你的虚荣留出一点空间

The Totem Pole

By Tao Zhijian

Translated from Chinese by Tao Zhijian

In slough and withered grass, on home land
Half of your trunk fallen, you stand
For what are you keeping watch
Like a frail elder, a candlelight
At wind's command
No longer are here brave hunters
Nor wives and kids expecting food back in the band
No longer do they need your protection
Nor do they need you —
To record their story, and fill their soul
With epic they best understand
No longer are there tepees around
To set you off glorious and grand
Nor to take you as witness of their story
Epitome of their life and land
No longer do they gather around you
To keep you company
And take your command
But, why did you not move
Like your brothers
To one of those charming and bustling parks
To adorn the scene, neatly built and planned?
There you could attract many eyes
Get into countless photos
And earn you

白金城市
远红日/ By Hongri Yuan

时间的五彩宝石啊
你铺成了光芒的天路
在一座星辰的王国
我找到了自己的家园
我打开一座座太阳的城门
在一座座黄金的城市
见到了一个个神圣的巨人
在那宝石镶嵌的皇宫
阅读了史前奇妙的诗篇
一部部古奥华丽的巨书
镌雕着黄金的词语
一篇篇玄奇美妙的故事
迷醉了我的双眼
我走进了一个个崭新的宇宙
看到了一座座圣洁的王国
在地球还没有诞生之前
曾经是人类的史前的家园

时空的水晶啊光芒闪耀
一座白金的城市矗立眼前
一只只飞船悠悠飘过
像一只只巨鸟五光十色

我看到一个个年轻的巨人
身体闪耀七彩的光环
他们的眼睛欢喜明亮
聚会在一座水晶的花园

他们唱着欢快的歌曲

跳着一种奇妙的舞蹈
一对对高大的少男少女
仿佛在庆贺盛大的节日

我看到一座圆形的巨厦
高高耸立在城市的上空
发出一道道白亮的闪电
高高地飞入宁静的太空

一座座通体白金的巨厦
构成了一个美妙的图案
整个城市是一个圆形
排列成一个精致的结构

我走进一座明亮的大厅
看到一排奇特的仪器
墙上悬挂巨大的屏幕
显映出一片金色的太空

一座座五光十色的城市
像一块块五彩晶莹的宝石
那些奇丽的高楼巨厦
胜过了人间幻想的神话

我看到一行行陌生的字母
在一面屏幕上匆匆闪过
几位年轻健壮的巨人
专注地观看变幻的图像

他们的神情宁静安然
两眼闪映智慧的光芒
穿着一种闪光的衣装

通体上下是一个整体

他们的身材异常高大
个个足有七米多高
男男女女容貌端庄
几乎没有年龄的区别

他们的皮肤洁白如雪
隐隐闪出亮丽的光泽
明亮的眼睛单纯如婴儿
又含着一种奇异的火焰

他们操纵神奇的仪器
变幻太空一幅幅图景
他们的语言简洁流畅
像钟磬一般悦耳动听

我端详这座明亮的大厅
感受到一种强大的能量
身心充满了幸福欢喜
自己也仿佛变成了巨人

我似乎听懂了他们的语言
他们在探索宇宙的奥秘
那一颗颗星球上的城市
住着他们无数个伙伴

他们用意念操纵仪器
也可以用意念传递信息
即使相距千里万里
也可以自由地用心交谈

那屏幕上的一行行文字
即是远方传来的信息
整个宇宙是他们的家园
他们在太空建造城市

他们乘坐的太空飞船
可以到达另外的空间
一瞬间化成一道闪电
在空中变得无影无踪

我感受到一种新的文明
他们长着神奇的眼睛
他们似乎能看到未来
也能进入不同的时空

男男女女都圣洁慈爱
胜过人间所谓的爱情
他们仿佛不懂得衰老
也不知道什么叫战争

时间仿佛并不存在
科学就是奇妙的艺术
他们的快乐来自创造
对宇宙充满神圣的感情

我看到一位年轻的巨人
打开了一座白金的大门
一座圆形的华丽的大厅
坐满了一排排男女巨人

我看到一座水晶的舞台
旋转在这座大厅的中央

一位端庄美丽的少女
演奏着一种巨型的乐器

一束一束金色的光芒
变幻出各种奇妙的图形
一种玄妙动人的音乐
仿佛是龙凤悠然的啼鸣

我看到一位健美的巨人
在台上跳出奇异的舞蹈
他手中托起巨大的圆球
球内闪耀着彩色的画图

我看到一队妙龄的女郎
穿着一种雪白的裙裳
他们仿佛在翩翩飞翔
像是一只只巨大的仙鹤

巨大的圆厅金碧辉煌
像水晶一般清澈透明
又像是嵌满奇异的宝石
闪耀出一种绚丽的光芒

我看到一位年轻的歌手
全身缭绕着金色的火焰
那声音奇特而又优美
像是歌唱又像是吟诵

他们的音乐欢喜玄妙
像一道道闪电变幻莫测
仿佛是宇宙的一颗颗星球
在太空中闪烁亮丽的光芒

又仿佛一座座水晶的城市
在空中矗立宏伟辉煌
无数奇妙的金色的花朵
开满了清澈晶莹的太空

我看到一张张透明的笑脸
仿佛是一座缤纷的花园
金色的光芒从天空洒下
化成了一座座黄金之城

我走出了这座圆形大厅
来到一条宽阔的街道
光洁的路面嵌满宝石
两旁林立白金的巨厦

在这儿没有人间的树木
却盛开各种奇异的花朵
浓郁芳香又闪闪发光
形成了一座座街心花园

这是一些奇特的花木
枝干透明仿佛水晶
闪烁各种奇妙的颜色
还有一串串金色的圆果

我看到一座巨大的塑像
仿佛一个太空飞船
高高地耸立在街头中心
周围闪耀一颗颗星球

我看到一柱柱晶莹的喷泉

在一座巨大的圆形广场
一座座造型优美的雕像
刻画出一个个圣洁的巨人

一座座巍峨壮丽的巨厦
环绕着这座圆形的广场
巨厦的上面是一些花园
还有一座座白金的尖塔

我看到一条宽广的河流
怀抱着这座巨大的城市
水底闪映出透明的金沙
还有一颗颗七彩的宝石

岸边排列高大的花木
和一条条水晶的长廊
一种色彩亮丽的大鸟
三五一群在水面飞翔

我看到一座广阔的树林
摇曳着一树树黄金的树叶
树林中耸立一座座尖塔
又仿佛一些白金的楼阁

我看到一些漫步的巨人
男男女女健美潇洒
或在水边或在林中
像鸟儿一般逍遥自在

奇妙的太空亮如水晶
怀抱着这座白金城市
一只一只白亮的巨球

在空中闪放无际的光明

仿佛是一颗颗巨大的太阳
又像是一颗颗人造的星球
整座城市也闪放光芒
形成一种神奇的景象

一种奇特的飞驰的列车
在城市上空回环往复
天空中仿佛有一种轨道
像一条银白闪亮的曲线

那一座座通体白亮的巨厦
仿佛是一座座神奇的迷宫
巨大的城市异常宁静
甚至听不到风儿的声音

我告别了这座白金城市
奔向了一片金色的太空
在这儿矗立另一座城市
一座巨大的黄金之城

这儿的建筑同样巨大
却是另一种美丽的造型
整座城市金光灿烂
黄金的巨厦美如雕塑

这儿生活着另一些巨人
仿佛来自另一个民族
他们拥有伟大的智慧
像黄金一般圣洁的文明
1998.3.3 北京

Platinum City
By Hongri Yuan
Translated into English by Manu Mangattu

Ah! Of iridescent gems of time
The heavenly road you paved light !
In a kingdom of stars,
I found my home.
In the golden cities,
I opened the gates of the city to the sun,
To behold the godly giants.
At the royal palace of the jewel
I read of prehistoric wonderful poems
The enormous, gorgeous ancient books.
Carved with the golden words
The wondrous strange mystery tales,
Made my eyes drunken.
I walked into a full new world,
And saw the holy kingdoms:
Even before the earth was born
The erstwhile home of human history.

In the crystal garden I saw
A crowd of youthful giants,
Their eyes were bright and glittering
In the aura of the body sparkle..

Across Time and Space in crystalline glitter
Stands this moment a platinum city
A ship drifting leisurely,
Like large birds, resplendent in variegated hues.

They sang happy songs
They danced a wonderful dance
Lanky boys and girls in pairs
As if to celebrate the splendid carnival.

I saw a circular edifice
High above the city.
Giving out white-bright lightnings.
Raised ground to fly into the quiet space.

A frame of platinum edifice
Creating a beautiful pattern.
The whole city is a circle
Arranged into a fine structure.

Into a bright hall I went.
A strange instrument there I saw.
A huge screen hanging on the wall,
Displaying a golden space.

Like bits of colourful crystal gemstones!
Resplendent with variegated colours of the city!
Those strange and beautiful high-rise buildings
A sight better than the myth of the world.

I saw lines of strange letters.
On one side of the screen flashed swiftly
Numerous young and strong giants
An effort to concentrate on the changing images.

Their look is quiet and peaceful.
The learned flame flashes in their eyes.
In a flash of clothes

The next is a whole.

Their stature, unusually tall.
Each one is well-nigh seven meters high.
Both men and women look dignified
Almost no age difference apparent.

Their skin is white as snow
With a faint flashy shine
Bright eyes are as naive as an infant's
Also kindled with a strange flame.

They manipulate the magic of the instrument.
A picture of the changing space.
Their language is artless and plane.
As the bell is generally pleasant.

As I survey the length and breadth of the bright hall
I feel a powerful energy
Body and mind suffused with bliss and delight.
As if I too am a giant.

I seem to understand their language.
They are exploring the mysteries of the universe.
The cities on a lot of planets
Peopled with their countless partners.

Their mind they use to manipulate the instrument
Also can to transfer data be used
Even thousands of miles apart
Also to talk free to the heart.

Many lines of text on the screen

Is but a message from afar.
The whole universe is their home.
They build cities in space.

They use the spaceships
To transport you to far-distant other spaces.
Into a lightning, a moment, and you
Vanish into thin air, without a trace.

I feel a new civilization.
They have magical eyes.
They seem to be able to see the future
And can enter diverse times and spaces.

Men and women are holy and loving
Superior to our world's so-called love
They don't seem to understand ageing
Neither do they know about war.

Time seems not to exist
Science is jut a wonderful art
Their happiness comes from the creation of
A universe full of divine love.

I saw a young giant
Opening the door of a platinum
A round, magnificent hall
Packed with rows of giants of men and women.

I saw a crystal stage.
Gyrating at the center of the hall.
Where a dignified and beautiful girl
Was playing a huge musical instrument.

A bunch of golden rays,
Shifting with all kinds of brilliant graphics
A mysterious and beautiful music
Like the Dragon leisurely crowing.

Thence I saw an enormous giant
Jump out of the remarkable dance onto the stage.
His hands held a huge ball
Which flashed with many colourful drawing .

I saw a group of young girls
Wearing a kind of white dresses
They seemed to fly lightly
Like the giant cranes.

The huge circular hall was resplendent
With clear, transparent decoration.
Like a bizarre gem of a full set,
Scintillating brilliantly in the light.

I saw a young singer
About the golden flame
The sound was strange and striking
Like singing , like chanting too.

Their music is at once mysterious and blissful
That shift randomly like the lightning
As if many planets of the universe
Shining bright and light in space.

The crystal city, aloft in space
Looks resplendent, magnificent

Countless wonderful golden flowers
Bloom and blush in that flawless space.

I saw an image of a transparent smiling face,
As if it were a colourful garden
The sky shed the golden light
And turned it into a city of gold.

I strode out of the circular hall
Came to a wide street with a smooth
Pavement covered with precious stones
And in line with the platinum edifice.

There are no terrestrial trees here,
But they are in full bloom.
Sparkling with rich incense,
Shaping a garden at the center of the street.

Some strange flowers were there.
The branches as transparent crystal
Flashing all kinds of brilliant colours;
And bunches of round golden fruit.

I saw a huge statue.
It was like a spaceship.
Clustered around by shining stars,
High above the centre of the street.

I saw the column of a dazzling fountain
In a huge circle in the square;
An elegantly modelled statue
Portraying a holy giants.

The soaring magnificent edifices
Ran round the circle square.
There were some garden villas
There was a platinum steeple.

I saw a wide river
Girdling this huge city
The bottom flashed with transparent gold dust,
Amidst which were scattered brilliant gems.

The planning of tall trees on shore
And a long crystal corridor
A big multi-coloured bird
Three five one group floated on the surface of the water.

I saw a vast forest
The swaying tree, a tree of gold
The trees with towering spires
And as some platinum Pavilion.

I saw some giants along the walk,
Some male and female bodybuilders.
At the water's brink or in the forest
Like birds carefree and relaxed.

The wonderful space was as bright as crystal
Embraced this platinum city;
A giant, white and bright ball
Flashing boundless light into the air.

It resembled the huge suns
And like the man-made planets
The whole city was shining too,

Weaving a rare breed of magic.

A strange speeding train circled
About the city back and forth;
There seemed to be a kind of track in the sky
Like a shiny silver curve.

They seated body white buildings
As f it was a dreamlike maze
This huge city was unusually quiet,
Could not even hear the sound of the wind.

I bade goodbye to the platinum city.
Near a golden space
Stands another city here
A huge city of gold.

The building here is also huge.
But it's another beautiful shape.
The whole city is glittering
Golden edifice as beautiful as sculpture.

Here there live some other giants.
As if from another nation
They have boundless wisdom.
Like a golden, holy civilization.
3.3. 1998

There Were Moments
By Emily Achieng'

There were moments
when a laughter meant happiness

There were moments
when calm meant peaceful

There were moments
when a smile meant satisfaction

There were moments.

그랬던 적이 있었다.

By Emily Achieng'
Translated into Korean by 이의영

웃음이 행복을 의미하는 순간이 있었다

고요가 평화로움을 의미하는 순간이 있었다

미소가 만족을 의미하는 순간이 있었다

그랬던 적이 있었다.

Былимоменты
By Emily Achieng'
Translated to Russian by Aizhan

Былимоментыкогдасмехзначилосчастье.
Былимоментыкогдаспокойствиеозначаломир.
Былимоментыкогдаулыбкаозначалоудовлетворение.
Были и такиемоменты.

Uncertainty
By Emily Achieng'

Sometimes a gentle word can terrify
Sometimes a small pat can scare
Sometimes an assurance can bring crowdiness of thoughts
Sometimes

Languages
By Emily Achieng'

I am just wondering
how languages beautifully belong,
The fashionable sound they make
when they leave our mouths,
or get written or printed
or just come into existence.

DISPATCH FROM HORIZON
By Wanjohi wa Makokha

We wish to forget the namesStill written on lines of windsWith the
ink of misty silencesDrawn from wells of blind eyes

We wish to forget the namesThat linger under black dawnThe sun
refusing to rise todayTo shed light on their graves

We wish to forget the names
That call from caves of heartsThat once occupied the holes
of these hillocks of skeletons

Yes, we wish to forget them allLong after they marched aheadOn the
plains of botched pollsTheir destination – democracy

Yet with each return of electionsWe, remember them, as
echoes...Whenever we hear our own names
on queues questing after them too

DAUGHTER OF THE LAUNDRESS

(After Antonio Jacinto's 'Poem of Alienation')
By Wanjohi wa Makokha

There are stains that litter the sky
Blocking away the beauty of plain
Tracing as if by fingers of heaven
The horizon of the eyes within us

Stains that are of unknown shapes
Sketched on the inner side of souls
Mapping hectares of thought areas
Inhabited by deeds without notes...

On the broken brassiere of her now
Spread as such on linen of liquid red
You hold the stain like grains of lands
You visited in dreams from dirty here

NB: A forth verse stood here. It left.
As she did. (writer's note)

OF HOMELAND AMIDST BEYOND
By Wanjohi wa Makokha

The cemetery sits on a culvertSolitude surrounds it as hedgeThe
creek of Time under it sips
Tiny drops of its fresh secrets...

A lone dragonfly hunts for matesFemales of its home faking
deathThere is no speech or breeze, hereSilent stands the sky, high
above...

From a broken minaret, now ochre,Flies shrapnel of the shelled
Quran...
Whence once came the call to Piety
Eloquently speak verses of silences...

a solitary maiden stands
By Archie Swanson

xian in 1994
i bought four paintings
tightly rolled
by a student of the arts
and to this day they grace my wall

four seasons they display
that's all
winter
spring
summer
fall

in one a solitary maiden stands
upon an elevated ledge
above a cloudy gorge

a waterfall cascades to rocks below
a summer sun
beyond blue peaks
adds hazy glow
green leaves bedeck a leaning tree

she always looks away from me
towards a winter of snow washed trees
towards an icy heart maybe
perhaps she sings the sweetest song
that no-one hears

or is it spring she now recalls

bursting blossoms
bird calls
melting snow
i do not know

or is the autumn in her mind's embrace
slow golding of summer leaves
browns and tans
majestic show
this draining of life's precious sap
the stirring of the breeze
detaching leaves
that tumble to the river face
and race along the coursing flows
down to the winking sea
to places only heaven knows

孤高の少女が立つ

By Archie Swanson

Translated into Japanese by Fumio Ueno

1994年西安にて
四枚の絵を買った
その絵を描いた学生によって
強く丸められていた絵
そして今日に至るまで私の家の壁を優雅に飾る

その絵は四季を描画する
冬、春、夏、秋

絵の中で孤高の少女が立つ
隆起した岩礁の上で
入り組んだ峡谷の上で

岩に滝が流れ落ちる
夏の太陽の下で
青い先端を越えて
ぼんやりした柔らかい輝きが加わって
緑の葉が傾いた木を飾り立てる

少女はいつも私から視線をそらす
木を洗う雪の冬の方向に
氷った心の方向に
多分、おそらく彼女は誰にもきこえない甘い唄を唄ってる

それとも彼女が呼んでるのは春？
溢れんばかりに満開の
鳥が鳴いている
雪が溶けている

分からない

それとも彼女の心を取り囲むのは秋？
夏の葉がゆっくり黄葉する
茶褐色に高褐色に
壮大なショー
生命の貴重な活力の消耗
呼吸の混合
葉っぱが落ちる
川面に向かって急に落ちる
それから流れの方に沿って競争して
瞬く海に落ちていく
天国だけが知っている場所

ombak indah rain

By Archie Swanson

watercolour hues
south sumatra sea
surf cracks
thunder claps
live coral reef
tropical drops
raucous water
corrugated curtains
dancing palms
drumming rain
thunder again
earth drinks

ombak indah rain

By Archie Swanson

Translated into Japanese by Fumio Ueno

水色の色彩
南スマトラの海
波が割れる
雷が鳴る
生きたサンゴ礁
南国の雫
騒々しい水
波形のカーテン
踊るヤシの実
ドラムを叩く雨
また雷が鳴り
地球が飲みこむ

Gwalior *
By Amitabh Mitra

1
the pigeons flew off today
with a piece of sky
rains washed down the
mosque tomb
its
untoward gaze
somebody
hastily patched
with
red and orange brocade
salwars with a hint of firdaus
at night we caught stars
through holes
kisses and eyes
that dared to stray
out.

2

today
another evening has come back
in its finery
streets coil back in languor
i smell an aroma
like distant footsteps
lying on a divan
behind curtains
hiding shadows of
once

small talk
once
tiny kisses
i wait
i wait.

3

let me go
i had told you then
your smile unleashed a sea
in the ravines
palaces were swept off
to a distant sky
and a painted afternoon burnt the fort
for ever
yes, we must all leave, you concluded
this reign has finally ended
to a long summer once it had brought us together
birds had flown off somewhere
our kisses stayed only with hurts
breathing against ageless stones
and a rainbow climbed an arid bastion
leaped to escape a promised
another day.

4

there is a river closing in on a
night of shifting blues
ascending the dark.
a cluster sky
clang closes the gates.

paths and palaces hurtle
merging on a silksheen touch.
your eyes take over the
suddenness of everyday
forlorn tantrums of a skin and
brittle memories rush in
before the fort
falls to a splintered dawn.

Gwalior is a city in Central India, known for its forts, palaces and its heritage.

Gwalior

By Amitabh Mitra

Translation into Japanese by Fumio Ueno

1.
今日小鳥たちが小さな空と一緒に飛立つ
雨がモスクの墓石を洗い流す
その予期せぬ凝視
赤やオレンジ色のブロケードで
誰かが慌てて修繕する
フィルダウス風のサルワール
その夜私たちは星をつかまえた
穴を通して
道から外れようとするまなざしと口づけ

今日
あの夜がかえってくる
美しい衣装をまとって
重々しい静けさに戻る螺旋状の道
距離を感じる足音のような
アロマの香りがする
ディバンに横たわって
カーテンの後ろで
影に隠れて
一度
短い会話
一度
そっとキス
待っている
待っている

3.

行かせて欲しい
あなたにそう言ってから
峡谷の中で
あなたの笑顔は海に放たれる
その場所は彼方の空へさらわれる
そして 色塗られた午後が要塞を焦がす
どこまでもどこまでも
そう、私たちはみんな行かなければいけない、
この統治がかつて私たちを一緒にした長い夏の終わりになる
ことを
あなたは結論づけた
鳥がどこかへ飛び去った
私たちの口づけは心の中だけに留まった
永遠の石に対する呼吸と
乾いた稜堡を登る虹は
約束のあの日に急いで逃避した

4.
闇が深まる青色へ移り変わる夜に
迫ってくる川がある
散り散りになる空
ガチャンと門が閉まる
道　　と　　宮　殿　　が　　ぶ　　つ　　か　　る
シルクの光沢を放って
あなたの目が毎日の表面の虚しい怒りの突然を引継ぎ
そして脆い記憶がどっと圧しよせる
要塞が分裂した夜明けになる前に

※Gwalioe は中央インドに在る、要塞や宮殿、で知られる街。

154

Jacob in Hebron
By Christina A Lee

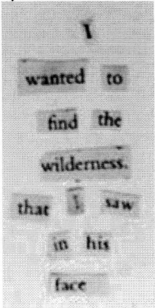

He told me I
could stay
until
the bone-coloured
morning

among
the dark, lofty
trees.

Yakobo wemuHeberoni

Namuzvare Christina A Lee

Kuturikirwa muChiShona nava Tendai Rinos Mwanaka

Ndaida
kuona
sango
Iro ndakaona
mumeso ake

Iye akandiudza
ndaigona kugara
Kusvika
kuchena kwamangwanani
kwakafanana noruvara rwemabonzo
Ruri mukati
mekusvipa kwemiti
mirefurefu

strange heights
By Christina A Lee

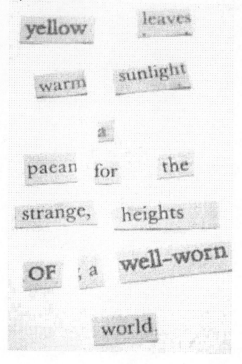

yellow leaves
warm sunlight
a
paean for the
strange, heights
OF ; a well-worn
world.

makomo emashiripiti

Namuzvare Christina A Lee
Kuturikirwa muChiShona nava Tendai Rinos Mwanaka

Mashizha ruvara rweghorodhi
Mwenje yezuva inodziya
Rwiyo rwokurumbidza
makomo emashiripiti
Enyika yasakara

African Heirloom
By Lind Grant-Oyeye

I have inherited her desires-
that yearning to hold lustfully
once again, dark sky lines. To draw lines
and patterns like a lover's stroke-
one for the time tears threatened to fill our eyes,
for what could have been.
A second one for burning heat
beneath the skin of another lover left yet
unfulfilled, while men are still weighed down
by precious stones stolen, from naked seashores.

Afrika Chishongedzo
Namuzvare Lind Grant-Oyeye
Kuturikirwa muChiShona nava Tendai Rinos Mwanaka

Ndakawana nhaka yezvishuviro zvemukadzi uyu
Kukungura kweruchiva rwokuda kubata
zvakare, miraini mitema yedenga. Kuda kunyora maraini
Uye mifananiso yakafanana netsvanzwadziro dzomudiwa
yokutanga yenguva masodzi aityisidzira kuzadza maziso
kushuvira zvaifanirwa kunge zvakaitika
Yechipiri yokutsva kwokupisa
Kuri pasi peganda kwouyo mudiwa akakusiya asi
Kusina kuzadziswa, apa munhu achingotsikirirwa pasi
Namatombo akakosha akabiwa, kubva kumahombekombe enyanza
isina kusimira.

Mourning
By Lind Grant-Oyeye

Is a field gone dark in the middle
Of this daily walk. We walked here
and talked about African violets -how
they were meant to outlast Autumns
and harmattans but their broken and fallen shrubs
now prick these soles, like the chills
of one left out in the cold.

Good bye Manaima
By Lind Grant-Oyeye

This is not a journey like any other-
Your lips like the tips of closed hibiscus bud.
We silently wish that you had opened
like a bold flower awaiting pollination or
some deity blessed at night, while men slept
Or danced with fevered rhythms.
Your laughter has become dulled by the sounds of sirens,
two minutes late and one scream short.

Wako wekutumbura
Nava Gumisai Nyoni

Ndewako here mwana waunowaridzira bonde?
Wakatumbura kupisira rusvava mujira?
Wako here wepamoyo waunoitira zino irema?
Kutarisa wako mwana woona murume?
Kuringa chako chimhandara woti mukadzi?
Imvi kuchena kuti ose majaya varume vangu?
Chokwadi here kuti amai isheche yevanakomana?
Kana vakavigwa nemakonzo woita chisodzi mate?
Ndimai rudzii vanorara mugota memajaya avo?
Kubereka rudzii kusina hunhu kubvisira mwana nhembe?
Kufumukai kunosemesa chero nenhunzi iri muchimbuzi?
Zvinorwadza sei mwana kuziva mai mukadzi?

For yours that you gave birth to
By Gumisai Nyoni
Translated into English by Tendai Rinos Mwanaka

Is that your child whom you spread a mat for?
You gave birth to burn the young tot inside blankets?
They are of your heart, you fake smiles for?
Looking at your son and seeing a mating partner?
Looking at your mature daughter and say a mating partner?
White haired to still say all the young men are mine?
Is this right for a mother to be a mating partner for boys?
When they are buried with mice your tears becomes saliva?
What kind of a mother who sleeps in young men's sleeping quarters?
What motherhood devoid of shame to strip naked for a child?
Meaninglessness so bad that sucks a fly that dwells in the toilet?
How painful for a child to know her mother as a mating partner?

Sevai Muto
Nava Gumisai Nyoni

Zvainokerekera zuva nezuva
Inogotingwaudza siku nesikati
Inogoumburuka mumadota kumhanyisa dzimwe
Ikatanga kuungudza nemachongwe anotama musha
Heyo pindikiti mumatendere edzimwe
Kupwanya adzo mazai hairegi
Yobudamo, kutoringa hapana rakandirwa
Kutoigadzirira rakaisvonaka dendere
Kutobata muromo jongwe, ibishi kudzifodora
Bva kukerekera uko kungoimba isingatambiki
Isheche rudzii isingazadzi churugwi
Zvairiyozve inozvitutumadza, ko mazai acho aripi
Zvainovhiringidza nejongwe remusha
Ko mazai acho achakandirwa zvadii
Tototya kuti muto tichatadza kuseva
Ikaramba iripo yoga muchurugwi
Hameno tikainzwazve kuchema nhiyo
Tinoda mazai kwete kukerekera
Ruzha urwo, nani tivese moto
Kuzoidya yachembera inogura meno!

Have its Soup
By Gumisai Nyoni
Translated into English by Tendai Rinos Mwanaka

As the hen clucks day by day
It disturbs us with noise day and night
Swimming and rolling in ash dust to disperse other
When it starts clucking even the cocks leave home
And then it enters other hen's nests
To break apart their eggs, it won't stop
When it comes out, when you check it has layered nothing
Even if you make it a beautiful nest
Waking up at cockcrow time, in the moment it belts
This clucking is singing of the impossible
What female that doesn't fill the hen's shelter
Since it preens its pride, so where are the eggs?
Since it terrorizes even the cock of the family
So when are the eggs going to be layered
We are scared we might never have soup
If it becomes the only one we are left with
We don't know we will ever hear a chick's cries
We want eggs not the clucking
That noise, its better we make a fire for it
If we wait until too old, eating it would hurt our teeth

Dundundu Nhando
Nava Gumisai Nyoni

Asi kurova dundundu padhibhi
Zvanzi rangu danga madhonza chete
Kurova chipfuva pakupura rukweza
Zvanzi dzangu ngavi ihamburamakaka
Kuzvitunhidza panhimbe
Zvanzi dzangu dzinosisa wakakodzekwa
Zvoyoferemuka imi mugere mumimvuri
Matumbu tashu, ko iyo dumbu hamuona kufovera
Zvayati rabada imi kushevedzera
Tora masora muvhare muromo ndima ifambe
Poyopoya ruzhowa, zvanzi torai muchiso ine musikanzwa
Ko kubuda furo hamunei nako
Ko mafuro zvayava kumasuwa hamuna ngoni
Muchatinhira riini kurwizi inopedza nyota
Saka chamunoda kudhonza kwayo
Kuti igutewo, chirahwe kwamuri
Kuona nenyanga dzoonda!
Bva kana yofushira chibage musakungura.

Fake Pride

By Gumisai Nyoni

Translated into English by Tendai Rinos Mwanaka

So they beat their chests at the dip tank
They say my kraal is filled up with oxen
Beating their side chests at harvesting of crops
That my oxen are the strongest ones
To be proud of oneself at the beer party
That my cattle milks full cream lactose
Now that it is apoplectic whilst you sit in shade
Ballooning stomach, that stomach- don't you see its constricted
Now it lies still whilst you call out
Take grass and stoke shut its mouth for cultivation to continue
When it breaks out of enclosure, you burn it on the face, it is difficult
That it is apoplectic, you don't care
Now that it isn't happy, you still have no mercy
When are you taking it to the river to quench thirst?
So what you are only interested in is draught power
For it to be nourished, it's an old tale to you
See its horns are also frail and thin
So when it makes you bury down crops don't be surprised

The precision of MEASUREMENT!
By Laxmeshwar

I understood how good you were
When you divided our short meeting
Into perfect QUARTERS
You were so aware of every hour that we spent —
Smoke, drinks, love-making and poetry - a quarter for each.
Like you could divide the day into perfection
And slot them out like waves ready to soar exactly after the other
You know when I fell in love with you —
Not in that instance when your crude hands
Held the joint for me
Or not when you scrambled the eggs with such focus that it seemed
as tough as art —
But in that moment when you picked your favourite book of
Kolatkar and recited Pi-dog,
I knew it had to be you
You breathed proportions.
Breaking up came easily to you
And you divided me precariously
Maybe you were getting too high, of late
Your hands were shivering
You didn't realise it then but you cut a piece of yourself and gave
away a chunk of your heart
That I carry in the darkness of my womb
Where you find me
Is where you will find your missing self

OMIA Kpakpa

Poornima Laxmeshwar taa

Translated into Idoma by Lemuel Ekedegwa Odeh

Nje igbegenp alphi[lea]
Eko naje Obataha ka 190 kpii
Ko ega ENE yili a
Aje Ejeji awa n'alg ge ba
Ge gw'utaba, eje, y'ih9tu mla ypi k'ichi
Olebeka ale echi ko dill a

Ogbia Openyl ne ge beche Ogbogba ga ye a
Aje eko num je ihotu kwuo an
Owe eko n'abo ogwuda kwu o bi akwutd gam
Mani eko na yoi wia aigwu mla ogbeyi gpgn
Amani eko na yoi je pkpa kolatkar yq\ je pi-dog
Nje ka awo ne
Owu ofu kwuo we alewa
Oko ike le ono tuon

Ake lum ko bobi

Ikohi igbihi igbihi ajea a-gbo je nwune
Abo kwuo gboo fie egbulu
Aje eko Oman, aman ale iyo k'epa ke
Kwu einehi k'otu kwuo gam ne yo ipu aje
dobu k'ipu kwum
Ega na mum a
Abo na ge m'iyo ne yoi bi a du a.

171

Tales of tequila
By Laxmeshwar

Shot one

I built you and I mean it. Love doesn't happen. Love is work and I have slogged enough. Breath by breath, flesh by flesh, tear by tear, ache by ache I sliced myself like a fish divides the water - to sail through and I also did some magic like that to be into you. Creased, crumpled, disintegrated, almost dissolved. Find me in the tiny spaces of your ego. I found a home there.

Shot two

For all the times when Spring stood out from Autumn, when the galaxies, black holes and every other unnoticed, irrelevance made perfect sense, while I wrote poems and words flowed with ease — uncomplicated and uninhibited; love made me a moron. I even wrote about the moon and flowers. Sigh!

Shot three

Somewhere I craved your absence. It is the rule - perfect muses are not meant to last. The non-duality seemed better a theory. The arithmetic could not resolve the equation issue. We could not place a triangle in a square.

Shot four

We broke up several times (8 times in 7 years). I asked you to put aside your thinking theories that you gained from philosophies that were bent to suit. I was already split. If only you had noticed...

Shot Five

The world went on while I howled through my night awaiting a dawn that never arrived. The world is fucked up. Love sucks! No more love for me. Period.

Shot Six

PASSOUT!

lab rats
By Rohith

numbers in statistics,
deviating curves, dots,
rectangles, circles,
ratios, percentages. em

our deaths are
reduced lengths,
our sadnesses
notches in lines,
corpses burnt in blocks
of a graph paper.

they can foretell
a probability of our
miseries, hunger
 and deaths.
we are an agreeable
round figure.
we are a well crafted
piece of research.

we are silent screams
in folds of paper.
in the language of power
we are lab rats.

makonzo emumba mesayenze
Nava Rohith

Kuturikirwa muChiShona nava Tendai Rinos Mwanaka

svomho dzezviverengwa
kurasika mukutenderera, chiperengo chokupedzisa
zvivakwa zvine mativi mana, denderedzwa,
patsanurwa, uhwandi hwechinhu muzvakawanda. kufema

rufu rwedu
inhanho dzakadzorerwa
kushungurudzikana kwedu
kunobvarukira mukati kunge miromo yemuseve iri muraini
mishakabvu inopiswa mumabhokisi
ayo ebepa resvomho dzemagrafu

avo vanoona zvirimberi
kuitika
kwekushupika kwedu, Nzara
nendufu.
tiri zvedu kubvumirana
kwechivakwa chakatenderera
tiri zvedu kuwumbwa kwakarurama
kwechidimbu chetsvakiridzo

tiri zvedu kuzhamba kwakanyarara
mukuvhara kwemashizha ebepa
mumutauro wakadzama
tiri zvedu makonzo emumba mesayenze

175

Hospital
By Rohith

written at government hospital in Anantapur

sun
is an ulcer
that
never
heals

moon
is a hole
punctured
by a dog's
howl

rain
is an incurable
disease

winds speak
the clairvoyant language
of doctors

leaves fall
like the last words
of dying

Where I come from...who I am....
By Smeetha Bhoumik

I am made of earth, trees, ancient
Birdsong and the enchanted river
Rispana that flowed past my grandma's
In Dehradoon. It now flows in my veins

Because when I came away it wouldn't
Be left behind! It flows on gently now
Singing those old favourite songs where
The hills danced around and the trees sang,

That is the real me deep within earth and
Skin. There are other outer layers that the
world views in parchments, documents, &
Mirrors, where reinforced concrete forms

My limbs, my hair is a halo of neon signs I
Find it hard to shake off, and the circles on
My wrists are social mores so old that it
Will take a lifetime to be free and done;

My home is a precious longing set amidst
Nostalgia and renewed birdsong moving
Towards skies of a new day, a new hope,
Somewhere very close to where you stay...

On the street if you see a frozen melody
Thawing out on sunny leaves and suddenly
ordering tea, you'll know it's me! There'll be
Skyscrapers dangling from both arms, but

Don't you mind them, they are such pile-ons!
(April 1, 2017)

Kwandakabva...zvandiri...

Namuzvare Smeetha Bhoumik

Kuturikirwa muChiShona nava Tendai Rinos Mwanaka

Muviri wangu wakawakwa nevhu, miti, nziyo
Dzeshiri pasichigare uye rwizi rwakakoshesesa
Rispana rwaiwerera kubva munambuya
Ku Dehradoon. Iko zvino rwavakuwerera mutsinga dzangu

Nokuda kwokuti pandakauya rwakaramba
Kusara kumashure! Ikozvino runowerera zvakapombodzwa
Ruchiimba nziyo dziya dzatinofarira paye
Zvikoma zvichitamba kutenderera uye miti ichiimba

Ndiye chaiye ini anogara mukatikati mepasi rino uye
Muganda rangu. Kune umwe hwaro hwekunze uhwo
Pasi rino rinotarisa zviri zvidimbu dimbu, magwaro, uye
Zviringiriso, apo zvivakwa zvakasimba zvaunganidzwa

Mipimbiri yangu, bvudzi rangu indenderedwa dema reratidzo itsva
Randirikutadza kusunungura mandiri, uye madenderedzwa ari
Chitsitsinhu chemaoko angu kufambidzana kwakanaka
kwepasichigare uko
Kuchatora upenyu hwangu hwose kusunungura uye kupedzisa

Imba yangu chigaro chokushuvira chakanakisisa mukati
mendangariro dzokushuvira uye kuwumbazwe nziyo dzeshiri
dzinofamba
Dzakananga kudenga rezuva idzwa, iri tariro itsva
Pamwevo pari pedyo nepedyo nepaunogara...

Munziri dzomudhorobha ukaona mimhanzi wezvakaomeswa
nechando

Wavekunyunguduka pamusoro pemashizha arohwa nezuva uye
pakarepo
Uchitenga putugadzike, unobva waziva kuti ndini! Pachava
Nechivakwa chinokwira mudenga chakabatirira mumaoko, asi

Usatya zvako ipapo, zvinhu zvinongounganira pamusoro pezvimwe
(Kubvumbi zuva rokutanga mugore remazana maviri negumi nenomwe)

What I See
By Smeetha Bhoumik

Multicoloured birds
Rainbows woven into dreams :
Tolerance kissing the sky.

If you'd told me a while ago there's no paradise,
Yes, I may have said, but today, oh, today how can I ?

Today, washed within its glow of sonnets, its scent
of words a river in flow, how can I, oh how can I?

Tell me you'll flow on forever thus, joining old wounds,
A Kintsugi touch and better than before, so how can I?

The birds flying all over the sky, freedom in their wings
They got me here, and they got you here, so how can I?

When you invited me in, you gifted me bits of the sky,
Some sonnets and birds too, so today, how can I?

No, today I shall hold back my nod, and only smile with
The day's unfolding, because today, how can I, oh, how can I?

I see you floating some thoughts away like shikaras, the
Water rippling in their wake, so today, how can I?

Today, just let me revel in your grace, and make it last forever...
(April 4, 2017, Haiku & Ghazal)

How I Wonder!
By Smeetha Bhoumik

In the flight of birds, do dead men's voices berth?
Afternoons in the sun, sparkle, confront, echo
That which couldn't be said, alive, oh

Now where would you put aside, words?

It's all over the sky, all over the bloom, the azure toe
Holding captive an errant squirrel, burrowing
Into cave-like cravings, ego, name, terms

Now where would you put aside, swords?

In the soil are roots, in the soil boots, unceasing
Rain, torso, hidden skeletons, frozen dreams
Maps rotting like putrid flesh, dead lines

Now where would you put aside, birds?

Do they fly frozen to extreme ends, words?
(April 10, 2017)

ONE WORLD
By Eniola Olaosebikan

Here today
We stand
In the beauty of nature;
No race, no class, no tribe.

We share with ourselves
Our nature given gifts-
Our smiles and hugs.

We share our affection
Laden with no shame, guilt or fear,
We stand
As the hope of a world long lost.

Here today
We stand shoulder to shoulder,
Leaning in love on love.
We rid our hearts of the hatred and sorrows of yesteryears
And present it to another,
As the Creator gave us-
Pure, innocent and sacred.

Here today
We spread our warmth to the dying world
Like bright shining warm fires
And we leave here
With such love shared;
We leave here-
One world.

II
Here today
We stand-
One world
One hope
One love.
We stand
Without a name-
No African, no American, no European, Asian, Australian or Antarctican.
We stand without a race-
No black, no white.
We wreathe ourselves into history;
A history of love, peace, faith and affection towards one another;
A history of kindness, compassion and hope;
Here in this great hall,
I am you
And you are me;
Together,
We are
One World.

Read at the Gala night of Aberystwyth university (Wales, United Kingdom) gala night 2015.

Motherland chant
By Eniola Olaosebikan

Arise Africa!
Arise in your glory and splendor,
Arise! In the light in which you were made.

Arise! Call your nations together,
Pass your strings through the holes, and
Play for us
A joyful melody.

Let us gather round the warmth of your fire
For lovely tales at moonlight.

Arise! Light our faces with joy!
Cause us to rest on each other's shoulders
In love and laughter,
As we hear at night by the fire
Stories from your lips.

Arise Africa!
Lest we be mocked by the world!

أنشودة الوطن

By Eniola Olaosebikan

Translated into Arabic by Fethi Sassi

إنيولا أولوسبيكان
الترجمة : الشّاعر فتحي ساسي

تحيا إفريقيا !!
تحيا في مجدك وفي انتصاراتكَ ،
في الضّوء الّذي خلقت منه .
فلندعو وطننا معا ،
ونمرّر السّلاسل من خلال الثّقوب ،
ولنعزف لنا لحنا جميلا ،
دعنا نجمع دفء حياتكَ ،
لحكايات جميلة على ضوء القمر .
تحيا لنضيء وجوها بالفرح .
ونرتاح على أكتاف بعضنا بعضا ،
في الحبّ والضّحكات ،
كما نسمع ليلا بحكايات حارقة من شفتيكَ ...
فلتحيا إفريقيا ..
حتّى لا يستهزأ هذا العالم منّا .

186

For colored only?
By Eniola Olaosebikan

I am no colored
But if ever by chance I am,
Then I color the world;
I hold the beauty of the world
In my hands.
Or tell me
Without colors
How would the world be?
Just bland?
If indeed I'm colored
Then I give the world
Its peacock beauty:
I am-
The spice of the world.
II
As rainbow is to the sky
I am to the world-
Its beauty.

للمتلوّنين فقط ؟

By Eniola Olaosebikan

Translated into Arabic by Fethi Sassi

شعر أينيولا أولاوسيبيكان
التّرجمة : الشّاعر فتحي ساسي

أنا لست متلوّنا ...
وإن كنت عن طريق الصّدفة كذلك ،
يمكن لي أن ألوّن العالم .
أحمل جمال هذا العالم بين يدي ...
ولكن قل لي دون ألوان
كيف يمكن أن يكون هذا العالم ؟
فقط دون طعم ؟
ولو كنت فعلا متلوّنا ،
سأعطي العالم جمال الطّاووس
فأنا بهار هذه الدّنيا ،
مثل قوس قزح في السّماء .
أنا جمال هذا العالم ...

Roots
By Vinita Agrawal

My ancient words,
self mutilated...
moving beneath me
in my veins and muscles
or just sitting in my eyes
like skulls of birds

These words, my heritage
sun themselves on the mind's terrace
like turmeric coated raw mango slices
I seek to lacquer them with gold leaf

I'm looking for Grandma's patois
a new heaven, a new earth
I want to scrape them clean of rust
I want to bring out ethers snuffed by the sun
I want to bring alive the fulcrum of an embrace.

I am lost in an acquired language
It smothers me like moss and lichen
My lineage grunts
I feel a riverbank drying.
My lips part into a map of thirst

I want to speak like my ancestors did
Inhale once more, the lingering incense of their words,
At the edge of paved stones

Come back... my heritage,
Come back disguised as a tree.

Keep me in your shade
I'll polish your every leaf
Come back wearing morning's clear light
at my naked window.

Midzi yedzinza

Namuzvare Vinita Agrawal

Kuturikirwa muChiShona nava Tendai Rinos Mwanaka

Mazvi angu echinyakare,
Anozvidimbura pachavo...
Kufamba pasi pangu
Mutsinga dzangu uye Munyama dzangu
Kana kungogara zvavo mumaziso angu
Kunge hodigo dzeshiri

Mazvi aya, upfumi hwangu hwamangwana
Anozvidziyisa nezuva muzvigaro zvepfungwa
Kunge zvidimbu zvemango dzisati dzaibva zvakarungwa neupfu hwetsangamidzi
Ndoda kuzora Mushonga weLacquer wemivara yeghorodhi

Ndinoda kutsvaga Mbuya vangu ndimi dzepasipasi
Denga idzwa, nyika itsva
Ndinoda kudzikwenga kusvika dzachena ngura
Ndinoda kubudisa mhepo dzepamusoro dzabiwa nezuva
Ndinoda kuunza simba rese rokumbundirana

Ndarasikira mumutauro wokudzidziri
Unondimomotera kunge zvimiti nezviuswa zvidikidiki zvinomera padombo
Zvizvarwa zvangu zvichakungura
Ndinonzwa mahombekombe erwizi achioma
Miromo yangu ichivhurika kuva nyika yenyota

Ndinoda kutaura kunge mudzimu
Kusweta zvakare, hwema hweinisenzi dzemazvi asaririra
Pahwaro hwetumatombo twakarongwa munzira yokufambira

Huya zvakare… upfumi hwangu hwamangwana
Huya zvakare wakazvihwandisa semiti
Ndichengetedze mumvuri mako
Ndichadzuru nokushainisa ripi shizha rayo
Huya zvakare wakapfeka rujeko rwakachena hwamangwanani
Pahwindo rangu rakashama

Black Waters
By Vinita Agrawal

The revolutionaries were exiled for life
in a puce colored colonial prison
on an archipelago, untraceable on the maps.
Every breath harrowed, black-hued or not at all.

Iron contraptions for the neck and ankles
Coarse jute tunics for torsos.
Rations - fit for sparrows
Flogging that made buttocks bleed.
Permitted to urinate just once a day.

Tortured and abused on hand-driven oil mills
extracting 10 lbs of coconut oil, like an indemnity.
Their nerveless hands slack, their countenance fractured.
Up in the heavens, stars glistened moistly for these rebels.

No one ever escaped these Black Waters, the excruciating seas, the
agonizing oceans.
Only their screams made it out. Raided the air,
cracked the winds and lay scattered like dead leaves on the islands...
like fragments of a tormented mind.

To think that political dissent could be like this.
Indictment could be like this.
That a man might lose all dignity, die of hunger, lose his mind,
be crucified at the edifice of endurance but gain a country,
nevertheless.

Writers Without Borders
By Vinita Agrawal

Rain waters listen to secret flowers beneath the soil
The night settles to darken the bottoms of trees
My ink flows, mingles without geography.

Every tear fills the jar of the waiting moon
And despite the hell-towers all around
Writers resurrect the doors of broken thoughts.

Every star branch trickles with blood's bitterness
War reigns across borders, land fights land
Religion versus religion. Everywhere, a divided stand.

Yet, my fellow pen, fellow nib, fellow hand
Though the needle of pain pierces your darkened veins
Write! So that man may understand man.

Write sans borders, fences, frontiers
Make thick the river of sentiments
Call swiftly for peace, for love.

History doesn't change that fast
Time doesn't bend easily
Change doesn't happen overnight.

Still, the votives of clattering flowers
Fall gentler on the chest of pebbles
The sun comes out again...because of words of dissent.

Tremors of joy run through your fingers
As darkness builds a dawn

Write on!

For countries war torn,
Let darkness build a dawn
Wherever you are...Write on.

With This Pen
By Edward Dzonze

With this pen
I intend to move people and mountains
beyond their geographical enclave ,
I intend to ignite the fire
extinguished by the tears of literary critics
who corrupted writers with partisan politics.
I intend to silence gunshots from the African wilderness
with the wise words of bitter guerillas
whose blood strewed the African turf in rebellion of colonialism
I intend to do so much under the sun ,
I intend to do so much with this pen

Excuse me ,
I'm not leaving a page blank
So much life around me,
I'm painting pictures
that move along with people in the African ghetto streets,
shadowy pictures ahead of days and the people
life size portraits of our achievements and follies,
I'm here to provoke the blindness
that saw Azania take charge against Bantu children in a xenophobic
stampede,
I intend to do so much under the sun
I intend to do so much with this pen.

With this pen I'm digging deeper,
deeper beyond the surface of graves
in search of the bitter and sweet truths
that escaped or nature down ancestry
I'm walking deserted alleys and pavements

scavenging for the stench of stinking truths buried in dustbins
I'm singing a familiar song
with an unfamiliar voice;
Be warned, the unfamiliar voice might capture the chorus better
If it's the song and not the voice that matters;
With this pen in hand
I intend to do so much under the sun,
I intend to do so much before I run out of ink.

بهذا القلم

By Edward Dzonze

Translated into Arabic by Fethi Sassi

شعر إدوارد دزونز

التّرجمة : الشّاعر فتحي ساسي

بهذا القلم ،

أعتزم أن أحرّك النّاس والجبال ،

أبعد من منطقتهم الجغرافيّة ،

أعتزم إشعال النّار ،

لتطفئها دموع النّقاد ،

الّذين يفسدون المبدعين بالسّياسة والأحزاب .

وأعتزم إسكات الطّلقات النّارية في البريّة الأفريقيّة ،

بالكلمات الحكيمة من الحروب المرّة ...

الّذين نثرت دماؤهم الأراضي الأفريقية من تمرّد الاستعمار .

أعتزم أن أفعل الكثير تحت الشّمس،

أعتزم أن أفعل الكثير بهذا القلم .

عفوا ، أنا لا أترك صفحة فارغة ،

كثيرا من الحياة حولي ،

أرسم لوحات ،

تتحرّك جنبا إلى جنب مع النّاس في شوارع الغيتو الأفريقيّة ،

صور غامضة أمام النّاس والأيّام .

صور بالحجم الطبيعيّ من إنجازاتنا وحماقاتنا ،

أنا هنا لإثارة العمى ...

الّذي رأى " أزانيا " تتحمّل " أطفال البانتو " في كره ذريع للأجانب ،

أعتزم أن تفعل الكثير تحت الشّمس

أعتزم أن تفعل الكثير مع هذا القلم ...

مع هذا القلم أنا أحفر أعمق،

أعمق من سطح القبور ،

بحثا عن الحقائق المريرة والحلوة ،

الّتي تسرّبت أرضا أسفل السّلالة ...
أمشي هاربا بين الأزقّة المهجورة والأرصفة .
أبحث عن رائحة لحقائق نتنة مدفونة في صناديق القمامة .

أنا أغنّي أغنية مألوفة ،
بصوت غير مألوف ،
كن حذرا من الصّوت الغير مألوف الّذي يلتقط الجّوقة أفضل .
فالأغنية وليس الصّوت الّذي يهمّ ...
مع هذا القلم في متناول اليد ،
أعتزم أن أفعل الكثير تحت الشّمس،
أعتزم أن أفعل الكثير قبل نفاذ الحبر .

Poetry Cookies
By Nalini Priyadarshni

You want me to arrange my words
mold them in certain ways
because you say certain shapes are important
to make poetry more beautiful, and those
who get these forms right are masters
You wish me well when you ask me to
shape my expressions with cookie cutters
to make them look like those of old masters
I, being more concerned with texture
of ingredients I mix and slap into place
and the flavor they lend to my poems
can't be bothered with shapes just now.
Maybe I am just being stubborn
flailing my dough around and waiting
for the poems to grow organically
Or maybe I am intimidated by the task
of dusting my fingers with rhymes to
discipline words in a certain shape
But I want you to relish my poems
as they dissolve in your mouth
excite your palate, making you ask for more
for poetry is mostly about flavor not shape

Kashata za Ushairi

Na Nalini Priyadarshi

Translated into Kiswahili by Wanjohi wa Makokha

Unahitaji nipange upya maneno yangu
niyafinyange kwa namna fulani
Sababu wasema umbo fulani ni nyeti
Kufanya ushairi uwe wa urembo na
wawezao umbo hizi ndio wao magwiji
Unanitakia kila la kheri uniulizapo
Kutengeneza mistari yangu kwa kisu
cha kashata kuyaremba yafanane na
ya magwiji wale wa kale.
Mimi ninayezingatia manthari,
ya viungo nazichanganya haswa,
 hadi ladha zipeazo mashairi yangu,
hazitilii maanani mambo ya umbo tu
Pengine mimi ni msumbufu tu
nikifinyanga mali ghafi haswa
nikisubiri mashairi haya yaote
Au pengine nina mashaka na fani hii
kutumbukiza vidole vumbini kwa vina
ili kuunda aina ya umbo iliyo na ubora
Ila naomba uyafurahie maishairi yangu,
zinapoyeyuka mdomoni yako, zikidatisha
kinywa chako, hadi uombe uongezewe tu
Nakariri kuwa mashairi ni ladha tu wala sio umbo

Love We Deserve
By Nalini Priyadarshni

He sent her, his journeys
to her heartland
wrapped in 52 silk Ganeshas
hand woven in Banaras
that for decades witnessed, in silence
hashish induced visions
he filled his notebooks with or
puzzled over the meaning of barbells
ancients etched with ocher

AUM EKDANTAAY VIDMAHE

Long hours rolled between his fingers
translating into poems
for blue eyed lovers he longed for
under the watchful eyes of elephant head
munificent on brocade lotus
the granter of unsaid prayers
harbinger of wealth and good fortune
who missed staple of motichoor laddoos
and dreamt of a dusky lover for him

VAKRATUNDAAY DHEEMAHI

He sent her echoes of his footsteps of
years of backpacking across five continents
tucked in a leather pouch with blue buttons
of sun and moon bought from a hippie
and Ganpati pendent he never wore
but left where he could see it every day

bought in orient for his love for the divine tusker
A love he would share with his kohl eyed lover

TANNO DANTI PRACHODAYAT

And when coins were cast
hexagram 14, emerged out of years of fog.
If they could get past everything they had known
have faith in unseen, unheard and unfelt
seize the day, pour gratitude and healing into other's cups
the deepest love they deserved was theirs to claim.
Yellow Ganesha he picked for her birthday
rests lightly against her dark skin as
an unspoken vow to be renewed every day

AUM SHANTI, SHANTI, SHANTI

Penzi Tustahililo
Na Nalini Praiyadarshni
Translated into Kiswahili by Kariuki wa Nyamu

Alimtuma safarini
hadi vilindi vya roho yake
iliyofungiwa hariri hamsini na mbili za Ganesha
zilizofumwa kutoka Banaras
ilishuhudia kwa miongo, katika ukimya
uliosababisha maruerue
akiyajaza madaftari yake
au akishangazwa na maana ya miimo
iliyosimikwa kale kwa ngeu

AUM EKDANTAAY VIDMAHE

Masaa marefu yalijikokota baina ya vidole vyake
yakijifasili kuwa mashairi
kwa wapenzi wa thamani aliowatarajia
chini ya ulinzi imara wa jicho la tembo
Karimu wa hariri nzito, furaha na starehe
ajibuye dua lisilotamkwa
ishara ya ukwasi na ustawi
Alichelewa kula keki aipendaye ya motichoor laddoos
huku akiotea mpenzi wake machweo

VAKRATUNDAAY DHEEMAHI

Alimtumia mwangwi wa nyayo zake
kwa miaka aliyozuru likizo kwenye mabara tano
akibebea ndani ya beti la ngozi lenye vifungo vya bluu
vya jua na mwezi lililononuliwa kutoka kwa muasi wa Ulaya
na kidani cha Ganpati ambacho hakuwahi kukivalia

lakini alikiacha mahali alipokuwa anakichunga
alimnunulia mpenziwe kutoka matlai kwa ajili ya pembe falaki
Penzi ambalo angeshiriki na mpenzi wake aliyejiremba wanja
machoni

TANNO DANTI PRACHODAYAT

Wakati kura ilipopigwa
heksagramu 14, zilizuka kutokana na miaka ya ukungu
iwapo wangelirudisha nyuma kila walichokijua
kuwa na imani kwa visivyoonekana, visivyosikika na visivyohisika
waifumbate hiyo siku, wamimine shukrani na uponyaji kwa vikombe
vya wengine
penzi la vilindi walilostahili lilikuwa lao wadai
alimchukulia Ganesha la manjano kwa sherehe ya kuzaliwa kwake
lilivyomchukua vyema kwenye ngozi yake nyeusi
ni kama kiapo kilichonyamaziwa kikahuishwe kila siku.

AUM SHANTI, SHANTI, SHANTI

Half Kiss
By Nalini Priyadarshni

Rare, illusive and pure torture
you can't possibly begin to imagine what
a half kiss is unless you've had one
One moment it's inside your mouth
melting your lower lip
you let out a barely audible gasp
and poof – it's gone
just as its flavor begins to hit you.
Sometime earthy, sometime peppery
but mostly bookish, as sinfulness should be
like a jug full of Feni on a lazy afternoon
Flighty and flagrant even on good days
a half kiss can seriously jeopardize
your search for happiness
Like a blob of gum you step on carelessly
it tends to stick to your soul
gnawing it silently
Half life of any half kiss is way longer
than regular kiss of any variety
typically, a lifetime

Nusu Busu

Na Nalini Priyadarshni

Translated into Kiswahili by Kariuki wa Nyamu

Ni adimu, ya dhahania na yenye kutesa
huwezi anza tu kuiwazia
busu nusu ni nini ila tu ulipate
Punde tu li kinywani mwako
likiyeyukia mdomo wa chini
kabla ya kutoa mtweto
na wee- limeondoka!
Ni ladha yake tu unayoihisi.
Wakati mwingine kidunia, mwingine huwasha
lakini zaidi ya kifasihi, enye madhambi
kama jagi iliyojaa Feni alasiri yenye uvivu

Kwa uwazi na udhahiri hata kwa siku njema
nusu busu linaweza kuhatarisha
kutafuta kwako kwa furaha
Kama tone la gundi unalokanyaga bila kujua
linanata nafsini mwako
na kuguguna kimya kimya
Nusu uhai wa nusu busu ni refu
kuliko busu lolote la kila wakati
kwa kawaida, uhaini wako wote

OPELE
By NURENI Ibrahim

Seek that which seems lost
In the bowels of mystery
Hidden is the divine
Displayed openly, yet cryptic

Why did the sacred totems run
With all their maleficent spirits?
Who ate the golden coins
With a meal of fowls, and goats
And concoctions of obscenities?

Perhaps the new divine
Lies in hidden codes

Of ones and zeros
In a cathedral full of webs

What if the *Opele* that run
Is now binary?

Opele means the string of beads used in consulting the oracle, Ifa

الخرز

By NURENI Ibrahim

Translated into Arabic by Fethi Sassi

الشّاعر : نوراني إبراهيم
الترجمة : الشّاعر فتحي ساسي

أن تبحث عمّا يبدو مفقودا
في أحشاء الغموض .
حيث يختفي الإله
ثمّ يبدو علنا، ويعيد الاختفاء ...
فلمَ تهرب التمّائم المقدّسة
مع كلّ أرواحها الشّريرة ؟
ومن أقتات العملة الذّهبية ؟
مع وجبة من الطّيور والماعز ...
يختلق الرّذائل ؟

يمكن أن يكون الإله الجديد ،
ذلك الذّي يكمن داخل الشّفرات المخفيّة ،
من الآحاد إلى الصّفر ...
في كنيسة مليئة بالشّبكات .
فماذا لو كانت تلك الخرز الهاربة متناقضة ؟

209

Portrait of the poet as young woman
By Chandramohan S

Her hair
Freshly harvested
      Dreadlocks off limits to combs.
      It is an unedited gospel of love.

Tresses like streams
Of eternal fire-
From the arsenal of her body.

Poems conceived in a celestial tongue
When stars align with cesarean precision.
It is our own language.

Her verses
Are neither left nor right aligned
Time zones hinge at every line break
Like sunflowers- un-aligned to the scorching heat.

Every evening, on her terrace ,
she lets her hair down and flies kite,
Her verses tell vivid stories
Stitched together in myriad colors.

Her verses gurgle like rivers let loose.
She never braids them
With her bare hands
Before a poetry reading.

When her poems are read

No boyfriend or pimp is allowed
Inside the reading hall.

Her kite, untethered to her surname,
Soars high, till it gets entangled with the stars.

Attempting to translate her poems
Is like making love to a capricious mistress.

Her curly, kinky stream of verses
Sway to the rhythm of her gait
Untamed by the clanging of her anklets.

Her book of poems,
a treatise on disheveled hair
and tresses on fire.

Picha Ya Malenga Kama Mwanamwali

Na Chandramohan S
Translated into Kiswahili by Kariuki wa Nyamu

Nywele zake
kama mavuno mabichi
    Nywele ndefu zimesokotwa na zisizochanika
    Ni injili ya mapenzi isiyohaririwa.

Nywele zake ndefu kama mito
Ya moto wa milele–
Kutoka kwa ghala la silaha za mwili wake.

Mashairi yaliyotungwa katika anga ya ulimi
Wakati nyota zinajipanga kwa upasuaji sahihi.
Ni lugha yetu halisi.

Beti zake
Kushoto wala kulia hazijapangwa
Muda hutegemewa kwa kila mshororo
Kama alizeti zisizopangwa kwa joto kali.

Kila jioni, kwenye kijia,
Yeye huachilia nywele zake zipeperuke kama tiara,
Beti zake husimulia hadithi waziwazi
Zikiungwa pamoja kwa rangi maelfu.

Beti zake zanguruma kama mito iliyovunja.
Hazisuki kamwe
Kwa mikono yake mwenyewe
Kabla ya ukariri wa shairi.

Wakati mashairi yake yanasomwa
Hakuna sahibu wala kuwadi anakubaliwa
Katika ukumbi wa mawasilisho.

Tiara yake, bila kufungwa kwa jinale la ukoo,
Inapaa angani hadi inaponaswa na nyota.

Kujaribu kutafsiri mashairi yake
Ni sawa na kufanya mapenzi na binti kigeugeu.

Mpindo na msokoto wa mtiririko wa beti zake
Huyumba kwa mdundo wa mnenguko wake
Usiothibitiwa na kelele za mbugi.

Vitabu vyake vya mashairi,
makala ya nywele zilizoachanishwa
na zinatiririka kwa moto.

THIRTEEN WAYS OF LOOKING AT A BLACK BURKINI

"I created the burkini to give women freedom, not to take it away ""-Aheda Zanetti

By Chandramohan S

1

Burkini is a language
Terrifying those ignorant of its text.

2

Cops patrol her tan lines
Like dams patrol
Rivers flowing above danger marks.

3

All you need is in that bag:
Change into a garment
More palatable for the cops in uniform.

4

Some garments cling too close to your surname
Like a metaphor
Too loud for good poetry.

5.

Sea surfing can be tiring
Like an infinite ebb and flow of a questionnaire.
Batting an eye lid can be a tad too immodest.

6

Tether yourself close to the beach.

Do not surf too deep into the ocean.
Never self-intersect in circles of knots and tangles.

7

Bruises sustained from frisking
Metamorphose into festering wounds.
Gangrene could gnaw at your surname.

8

Erase your footprints from the sands.
Waves of time rarely wash the footprints of a scuffle.
Prolonged scuffle can bury us all in a deep hole.

9

Do you remember the first corpse
The sea sucked off a turbulent beach?
The sea spat it out after three days of frisking.

10

The footprints of scuffle
Implicates you from shore to shore,
Blowing up all bridges between you and anyone.

11

During this conversation
Some territory has been ceded across
The tan lines of your body.

12

Your body stripped of the garment
Remains an evacuated language.
Can a language be a scarecrow?

13
History will catch up with you
In your rear-view mirror
Even if you are full throttle in your
Pursuit of happiness.

NJIA KUMI NA TATU ZA KUTAZAMA BURKINI NYEUSI

"Nilitunga Burkini ili kuwapa wanawake uhuru wa kutoichukua" <u>Aheda Zanetti</u>

Na Chandramohan S

Translated into Kiswahili by Kariuki wa Nyamu

1

Burkini ni lugha
Inayotishia wanaopuuza tungo zake.

2

Askari wanashika doria wakilinda mipaka yake
Kama wanavyoshika doria mabwawa
Mito ikiteremkia juu.

3

Chochote unachohitaji kimo mkobani huo:
Badili uvae vazi
Lililo tamu sana kwa askari waliovaa sare.

4

Mavazi mengine yanajibana kwa jina lako la ukoo
Kama sitiari
Yenye sauti kubwa kwa ushairi bora.

5

Kuelea mawimbini inaweza kuwa na uchovu
Kama kupwa kusikorudi na mtiririko wa hojaji
Kupepesapepesa kope kunaweza kosa staha.

6

Kaa karibu na ufuo wa bahari
Usijongee sana kilindi cha bahari
Usiwahi jikingamanisha katika mizunguko ya mafundo na vitata.

7

Majeraha yatokanayo na upekuzi wa huku na kule
Yamesababisha vidonda vinavyotoa uvundo
Donda lingeguguna jina lako la ukoo.

8

Futa nyayo zako changaraweni
Mawimbi ya wakati si kawaida kuosha nyayo za vita
Vita vya muda mrefu vyaweza tuzika katika shimo refu.

9

Unakumbuka mwili wa kwanza
Ulioletwa na mawimbi kali hadi ufuoni
Bahari ikautapika baada ya siku tatu za kuusaka.

10

Nyayo za vita
Zakwandama ufuo hadi ufuo
Kulipua daraja zote zilizo kati yako na wengine.

11

Katika mazungumzo haya
Maeneo mengine yametwaliwa
Mistari ya mwili wako.

12

Mwili wako ukitolewa vazi hilo
Unabaki lugha iliyohamishwa

Lugha yaweza kuwa sanamu ya kuwinga ndege?

13
Historia itaandamana nawe
Kwenye kioo chako cha nyuma
Hata ikiwa unafanya hima katika
Juhudi zako za kusaka faraja.

Beef poem
By Chandramohan S

My harvest of poems
will be winnowed.
if done deftly,
the lighter shallow poems
 blow away in the wind
while the heavier, meaty poems,
 fall back onto the tray,
to become the fire in my belly
like beef.

Shairi Nyama
Na Chandramohan S
Translated into Kiswahili by Kariuki wa Nyamu

Mavuno yangu ya mashairi
Yatapepetwa.
Na ikiwa yatafanywa kiusanii,
mashairi mepesi yasiyo na uzito
yatapeperushwa na upepo yatokomee
ilhali yenye uzito, yaani mashairi yenye nyama,
yataangukia tena kwenye sinia,
ili yawe moto tumboni mwangu
kama nyama.

ROBERT MUGABE STREET
By Phumulani Chipandambira

urchins litter the street
and tout
along the pavements.
the madman urinates
at the walls
as he sucks the glued papers.
car brake screeches,
beggars shout
displaying their placards.
flies parade the pavements
and march
to a heap of rotten apples.
the strapped baby cries
startled by the ambulance hoots.
prostitutes expose thighs
and vendors jingle wares,
fleeing the marauding police officers.

on the streets of Harare
everyone competes for a space.

*The following translation from English into Idoma by Lemuel Ekedegwa Odeh

ULAYI U ROBERT MUGABE

Phumulani Chipandambira taa.

Ayi otowodo mla ayi ikpala

b'ulayi ẹbẹbẹ

ba ye okwonu ọwẹ

ojele ke yọi nma enchile bọọ dọ

le epu ọkpa w'okwonu yọi

pla nyẹ

ubleki ku moto yọi ya uya

aọba ọda yọi d'ẹgba

yọi ma ọda ne bia fu

iju omomu okwonu ọwẹ

ke ye ga

pe kwu owa ka apuu

oyi ne ba ọnya yọi jikwu

oyọi y'ufi ẹgba ka amblasi

a akwuna le atakwu

kpo bẹchẹ

a obi ọla hala bai bi ọla

kwua hala

bai kwu inya aidaha ṅda ne

bai gba jẹ ulayi ku Harare

DAMBUDZO MARECHERA
By Phumulani Chipandambira

He brooded the words
and he
let them hatch,

his words
breathed into life,
his words
are now scattered everywhere,

Let us all create the WORDS.

***The following translation from English into Idoma by Lemuel
Ekedegwa Odeh**

DAMBUDZO MARECHERA

Phumulani Chipandambira taa

oka ẹla yọi ipu

ok e chẹ lọ

le he w'ẹchẹ

ẹla kwunu

ọle owufuto

ole oyei lẹ

ẹla kwunu

yo ẹga doodu baba

alọ lẹ ẹla ya

A WRITER'S PEN
By Kariuki wa Nyamu

A writer's pen is extremely potent
thus Alex La Guma was persecuted
over words, words, words!

A writer's pen is extremely potent
thus Chinua Achebe fe$_{ll}$ in$_{to}$ m$_e$s^s in Biafran war
over words, words, words!

A writer's pen is extremely potent
thus Wole Soyinka was declared Wanted, Dead or Alive
over words, words, words!

A writer's pen is extremely potent
thus Sembene Ousmane faced wrath of French Senegal
over words, words, words!

A writer's pen is extremely potent
thus Ngugi wa Thiong'o was incarcerated devoid of trial
over words, words, words!

A writer's pen is extremely potent
thus Jack Mapanje was confined_in Mikuyu for years
over words, words, words!

A writer's pen is extremely potent
thus even valiant Idi Amin Dada shuddered with fear
over words, words, words!

A writer's pen is extremely potent
thus Ken Saro- Wiwa was ~~assassinated~~
over words, words, words!

A writer's pen is extremely potent
thus Micere Githae–Mugo had to go in$_{to}$............................exile
over words, words, words!

A writer's pen is extremely potent
thus Ben Okri was cast ^{off} from his land of birth
over words, words, words!

A writer's pen is extremely potent
thus Stella Nyanzi went through State repression
over words, words, words!

Oh lover of words, what on earth is mightier than a writer's pen?
That one and all marvel at the **AUTHORITY**
of words, words, words!

Nevertheless, won't this writer's pen m$_e$s^s me one day?
So that I may either be silenced forever
or live to tell tale behind bars
over words, words, words?

AL{ALAMIN MARUBUCI

Daga Kariuki wa Nyamu

Translated into Hausa by Abdulrahman S. Waziri and Mustapha Tanko

A}alamin mai yawan hikima
Haka, Alex La Guma ya tsananta
Bayan wasu kalamai, kalamai, kalamai!

Al}alamin marubuci mai hikima
Haka Chinua Achebe a ya}in biyafira
Bayan wasu kalamai, kalamai, kalamai!

Al}alamin marubuci mai yawan hikima
Haka. Wole Soyinka Aka neme shi mace ko a raye
Bayan wasu kalamai, kalamai, kalamai.!

Al}alamin maruci mai yawan hikima
Haka Sembene Ousmane ya fuskanci hushi na Faransa da Sanigali
Bayan wasu kalamai, kalamai, kalamai.!

Al}alamin marubuci mai yawan hikima
Haka Ngugi wa Thiong'o ya yi gida yari
Bayan wasu kalamai, kalamai, kalamai!

Al}alamin marubuci mai yawan hikima
Haka Jack Mapanje aka ha]a shi a Mikuyu na tsawon shekaru
Bayan wasu kalamai, kalamai, kalamai.!

Al}alamin marubuci mai yawan hikima
Haka ko Idi Amin Dada ya firgita
Bayan wasu kalamai, kalamai, kalamai.!

Al}alamin marubuci mai yawan hikima

227

Haka Ken saro- Wiwa aka bad da shi
Bayan wasu kalamai, kalamai, kalamai.!

Al}alamin marubuci mai yawan hikima
Haka, Micere Githae-Mugo aka barranta shi
Bayan wasu kalamai, kalamai, kalamai.!

Al}alamin marubuci mai yawan hikima
Haka Ben Okri aka kaushe shi daga mahaifansa
Bayan wasu kalamai, kalamai, kalamai.

Al}alamin marubuci mai yawan hikima
Haka Stella Nyanzi ya samu 'yanci
Bayan wasu kalamai, kalamai, kalamai.

Ya kai masoyin kalamai, menene a doron} asa ya fi } arfi fiye da
kalamai?
Duk wannan iko ne daga **HUKUMA**
Bayan wasu kalamai, kalamai, kalamai.!

Ko ba komai ka bar mini al}alamin marubuci wata rana?
Wata kila na yi shuru har abada
Ko a raye na fa]i labarin da ya gabata
Bayan wasu kalamai, kalamai, kalamai.!

If I may inquire…

(Inspired by my professor and mentor, Dr. JKS Makokha aka Wanjohi wa Makokha)

By Kariuki wa Nyamu

If I may inquire
who on earth shall spΟt the clandestine sod
that hid he who paid a dear price
of our Uhuru, with blood and flesh?
So that, we may perhaps concrete his grave
erect a scenic granite cross
set a heroic epitaph
place precious marbles
and lay a splendid wreath
in honour of most charismatic field marshal,
who loved our land selflessly
that he went through hell in our stead
in vile hands of Nyakeru!

If I may inquire
what science shall we exploit
to cheer up deprived widows of Mau Mau
who unremittingly weep, up till now!
Like Rachel of Testament
they've mulishly declined to be consoled
upon losing countless offspring in the fight back
and their tomorrow too!

If I may inquire
who'll unflinchingly pinpoint the slayers
of the smart and vociferous
lion of the Lowland
who was inexplicably gunned down on government road

229

thus hushed forever?

If I may inquire
how best can I make plain to our brood?
When history states
that their vocal grandpa's remains
were unearthed by a herdsman in forest?
What report shall I table
now that they ask over and over again
'What fault had he executed?'

If I may inquire
what shall I spell out about the other venerated leader
whose charred remains were recovered on those hills over there?
Who'll elucidate to world over
on what made our forefathers bear such plight?
If I may inquire
who'll account for agony of true patriots
inside chambers of that once dreaded House over there?
Who'll head reconciliatory forum
of those incarcerated without a court hearing
following allegations of multiple counts of treason?

If I may inquire
who'll ever accolade
eminent men and women
who gallantly fought for multiparty and democracy
in body, speech and pen
for heaven and earth knows
that they're true makers of our nation
and then, the recent toxic chopper crash...
My goodness, who'll be allotted to convince Wanjiku
that 'twas just one of God's plans?

Anyway,
Might you have mistaken me for one who's sober?
        Oh dear, please dare not!
For I just thought of posing thousand nonsensical queries
to enliven our brew joint
as we customarily gulp _{down} *muratina* with clansmen
moments after our annual sacred circumlocution of
the Mountain of Kirinyaga
Mwene Nyaga's dwelling!

IN DA ZAN TAMBAYA

Daga Kariuki wa Nyamu

Translated into Hausa by Abdulrahman S. Waziri and Mustapha Tanko

In da zan tambaya
Wanene a doron }asa ke ~oye sirrin }asa
Wanda ke ~oye, wa ke biyan farashi
Daga namu Uhuru, jini da tsoka?

Don haka, watakila kankare ne kabarinsa.
Kafa a tsaye, an ratsa zane
Rubutu da kirarin jaruntaka
A wuri mai daraja da aka }awata
Sannan aka shinfi]a dukiya

Don karrama mafi karamcin babban hafsan sojoji
Wanda ya rungumi }asarmu ba da son kai ba
Ya tafi da duga dugansa a madadinmu
Miyagun hannaye na Nyakeru.!

In da zan tambaya
Wata kimiyyace ta amfane mu
Na mataki babba don kariya matayen Mau Mau
Wa]anda ba su bar hawaye ba har yanzu.!
Kamar irin su Rachel da aka jarabta
Sun buwaya, matu}a a ka durtsesu
Sun rasa matansu da 'yayansu a fa]ar da aka yi.
Haka makomansu gobe kuma.!

In da zan tambaya
Wanene ba zai ji tsoron nuna wa]anda aka kasha ba
Don gaggauta bayyana ra'ayin
Jarumin yankin kasa (Lowland)

Wanene ba zai iya bayyana ta~ar~arewar gwamnati ba
Haka, shuru har'abada.?

In da zan tambaya
Ta ya y azan yi sau}i ga 'ya 'yanmu?
Lokacin da tarihi ya bayyana
Da kakanninsu masu fa]a suka rage
Ba komai duniya sai dabbobi a dazuka?
Wani bayani zan kawo
Ya za su yi tambaya cikin tambaya
Wani kuskure ne yay i?

In da zan tambaya
Ya zan misalta girman]aya shugaban
Wa]anda suka shantake sun aka tsibiri daga can?
Wa zai kawo sau}i a duniya kuma.
Akan abin da magabatanmu suka kyautatu akai?

In da zan tambaya
Wa zai jure ra]a]i na gaskiyar masu kishin }asarsu
Cikin]akuna dake sa tsoro, gida dake can?
Wa zai jagoranci sulhunta taron
Na wa]anda suka yi gidan yari (prison) ba tare da shara'a ba
Bayan laifuka da yawan cin amanar }asa

In da zan tambaya
Wa za a karrama
Daga cikin maza da mata
Wanene jarumi da yay i fa]a da jamiyyu da dimokra]iyya
Daga jikinsa, zancensa da al}alaminsa
Domin kiyama kuma da doron }asa
Sannan su ne masu alamar gaskiya a }asarmu
Hakanan, ba jimawa aka farmusu......

Gaskiya ta, wa zai bayar don tabbatar wa Wanjiku
Wannan kawai daga nufin Allah ne?
Duk da haka,
Watakila kai mini kuskure domin wani mutum mai kima
Toh abin }auna, kar kai hushi!
Domin kawai yin tambayoyi marasa ma'ana
Don jan ra'ayi da ha]a ga~o~inmu
Da rike al'adunmu *Muratina*da danginsa
Da}i}an lokutan bautarmu na cikan shekara don bu}atu
Na daga dutsen Kirinyaga
Wurin zama Mwene Nyaga.!

Okot p'Bitek
By Kariuki wa Nyamu

Okot p'Bitek
one of Africa's most revered literary man
heroic Acoli mouthpiece
devoted defender of African languages and culture
meticulous don of Literature
whose charisma still live
you'll forever remain outstanding
for outstanding is you!

Okot p'Bitek
ever jolly father
skilled Cranes footballer
excellent choirmaster
passionate peace maker
resolute combatant for equity
ingenious diplomat
You, who ignited song tradition in Eastern Africa
Today, I want to let you know
that the ideals you stood for
as you penned *Song of Lawino,*
Song of Ocol,
Song of Malaya,
Song of a Prisoner,
and *Horn of my love,*
have emancipated Mother Africa.

Okot p'Bitek
You, whose assertive ideologies
stand solid to date
gallant political activist

visionary and zealous critic and author
ray of audacity, honour and conviction
mast of inspiration and selflessness
Okot p'Bitek
we'll emulate your majestic legacy
Time without end

Okot p'Bitek
Africa's foremost literary icon and philosopher
Your footprints are all over earth
For sure, you're larger than life
foresighted crusader of human rights
from vile jaws of oppressors
You're simply out of ordinary
for posterity knows you
for weaving Africa's literary basket
and world over shall without end revere you
here on earth
and in sky-land!

Okot p' Bitek

Daga Kariuki wa Nyamu.

Translated into Hausa Abdulrahman S. Waziri and Mustapha Tanko

Okot p' Bitek
Daga cikin] an afirika masanin ilimi
Jarumtakar Acoli abin sauraro
Wanda ya du}ufa don kare harsunar afirika da al'adu
Mai kulawa da adabi
Wanda kimarsa bata jirkita ba
Ka gawurta har abada
Kai ne gawurtacce.!

Okot p Betek
Shugaba na }warai
Mai hali na }warai
Jarumin mawa}a
Mai }awa da alamar 'yanci
Mai nazari da jajircewa da nagarta
Wanda babu ruwanshi da wakilcin }asa
Wanda ya ri}e al'adun wa}ar gabashin afirika.
Yau ina son ku sani
Wannan ra'a yi da kake kai
Kamar yanda ka aje *wakar Lawino*
Wa}ar Ocol
Wa}ar Malaya
Wakar Bursuna
Da }ahon }aunata.
Ya samar da 'yancin Uwar afirika

Okot p Bitek
Kai, wa suke da masaniya
Su jajirce zuwa yau

Jami'in siyasar a}ida
Mai hangen nesa da himman wallafa littafi
Maras tsoro darajarsa ta tabbata
Ya yi tsaye da bu}atuwar al'umma

Okot p' bitek
Za mu yi adalci, don }awata dukiyarka
Ba da kurewar lakaci ba

Okot p Bitek
Mafi yawan adabin afirika da falsafa
Sa}onka yaw a]e duniya
Tabbas ka yi fice a rayuwa
Hangen nesa da harha]a kindi na 'yancin 'yan adam.
Daga }kunci da }untatawa
Ka fito cikin sauki yadda aka saba
Al'umma masu zuwa su sanka
Don kyautata adabin afirika
Haka duniya ba za ta }ure maka ba
Ciki nan duniya
Da sararin samaniya.!

Knowledge
By Rochelle Potkar

Half of this world had its breasts cut, its entrails ripped, its bowels dismembered, its houses turned to grey dust, its night skies full of drones - shooting stars for blinking sirens, heavy metal descending, over-throwing everything termed 'home': familiarity, love, raison d'être, into thin air. Its women forced into whores, men sodomized or enslaved, babies kept to die.

The other half of this world is always surfing the high blues, reading novels about this half that has its breasts cut, its entrails ripped, its bowels dismembered, its houses turned to grey dust, its night skies full of drones - shooting stars for blinking sirens and missiles, heavy metal descending, over-throwing everything termed 'home': familiarity, love, raison d'être. Its women forced into whores, men sodomized or enslaved, its babies kept to die.

When the books with these stories grew into too many, restless, bespectacled filmmakers see movie opportunities. They make one film after another to get under the skin, of that other half of the world. They come up with art-installations, talk shows that run for whole years over the bestiality of power and politics. After the grand finale of such festivals, everyone made merry, but sleeps at 10, so no one has dark circles under their eyes. In the off-season, this half takes to snorkeling, paragliding, deep sea-diving and walking with the fish; they are bored of swimming.

In the other half of the world, sleep rips from under the eyes, nightmares unfurl with every second. When it was quiet and the men were exhausted over the mayhem and the killing, half-limbed beings crawl, reading scrapes and pieces of stories by candle flames near brown-papered windows. They read of blue oceans that swim with dolphins, of people on a perennial picnic, of film festivals, sculptures, monuments and art installations; of fiestas and pita bread, siestas and chapels. They read of smart cities, citadels, and probes sent to space to discover new planets for water, aliens, and new gravity. That was the only way they sleep - either smiling or weeping. Some of them who do not sleep draw pictures on their bullet-ridden walls of waves and boats, and air balloons, filling it with any color they could find – sometimes even their own blood.

Both halves of this world thus roll on their hinges, keeping in touch through books, and stories, reinterpreting and reinterpreting that which was not theirs.
Only when it got too excessive – too good or gruesome to believe, either half calls the other: a *contemporain mythology*.
It was heartening that these halves of the same times are at least literate and know about each other. They are not complete strangers.

Maarifa

Na Rochelle Potkar

Translated into Kiswahili by Kariuki wa Nyamu

Nusu ya ulimwengu imekatwa vifua vyake, matumbo yake yamepasuliwa, uchango wake umechanguliwa, nyumba zimegeuzwa kuwa mavumbi ya kijivujivu, usiku mawingu yamejaa muziki- nyota zikimweka kama ving'ora, vyuma vikiangukia, na kuporomosha chochote kiitwacho 'nyumbani': uzoefu, upendo, kusudi la pekee la kuwa hai, vyote vikitupiliwa hewani. Wanawake wake wakilazimishwa kuwa makahaba, wanaume wakilawitiwa au kutiwa utumwani, watoto wakiwachwa wajifie.

Nusu hiyo nyingine ya huu ulimwengu kila wakati inarambaza vina virefu ikisoma riwaya kuhusu hii nusu iliyokatwa vifua vyake, matumbo yake yakipasuliwa, uchango wake ulivyochanguliwa, nyumba zake zilivyogeuzwa kuwa mavumbi ya kijivujivu, mawingu yake yalivyojaa muziki- nyota zilivyomweka kwa ving'ora na makombora, vyuma vizito vilivyoangukia na kuporomosha chochote kiitwacho 'nyumbani': uzoefu, upendo, kusudi la pekee la kuwa hai. Wanawake wake walivyolazimishwa kuwa makahaba, wanaume wao walivyolawitiwa au kutiwa utumwani, watoto wao walivyowekwa wajifie.

Wakati vitabu vilivyobeba hadithi hizi viliongezeka, watengenezaji filamu huona nafasi za kutengeneza filamu. Wanatengeneza filamu moja baada ya nyingine ili kuizoesha nusu hii nyingine ya ulimwengu. Wanafumbua sanaa ya ufungaji, maonyesho ya midahalo yanayotawala miaka yote kuhusu ukatili wa mamlaka na siasa. Kilele cha hatima ya sherehe hizo humburudisha kila mtu, lakini wanalala saa nne, kwa hivyo hakuna yeyote aliye gizani. Wakati msimu wa utulivu, nusu hii hugeukia shughuli za michezo kama vile kuogelea vilindini mwa bahari kwa bomba la hewa, kuruka hewani kwa parachuti, kuogelea vilindini na kubebwa na samaki, iwapo wamechoka kupiga mbizi.

Katika ile nusu nyingine ya ulimwengu, usingizi unapasua macho yao, majinamizi huwatawala kila sekunde. Wakati wa utulivu watu wanapochoshwa na ghasia na mauaji, nusu yao wamelemazwa hadi wanatambaa tu, wanasoma vijipande vijipande na vijisehemu vya hadithi hizi kwa vimuri vya mshumaa karibu na madirisha ya karatasi za kikahawia. Wanaposoma kuhusu bahari za samawati zinazoogelewa kwa pomboo, kuhusu watu walioenda likizo za muda, kuhusu filamu za tamasha, vinyago, michongo, na sanaa ya ufungaji, kuhusu sherehe za mapumziko na dini. Wanasoma kuhusu watu miji mizuri, majengo marefu ya kifahari, na vichunguzi vikitumwa angani kugundua sayari mpya za maji, wageni na mvuto mpya wa ardhi.

Hiyo ndiyo njia pekee walivyoweza kulala wakitabasamu au wakilia. Baadhi yao wasiolala huchora picha juu ya kuta zinazoendeshwa kwa bunduki ya mawimbi na mashua, na purutangi za hewa wanazozijaza rangi zozote wanazopata- wakati mwingine hata damu zao.

Nusu hizi zote mbili za ulimwengu basi zinajisukuma kwa bawaba zao kupitia vitabu na hadithi, wakitafsiri tena na kutafsiri tena kile ambacho hakikuwa chao.

Ni wakati tu yalipozidi- yakawa mazuri zaidi au yakunata zaidi ya kuamini ndipo nusu moja ikaita ile nusu nyingine: mitholojia ya kisasa *(contemporain mythology)*.

Kilichotia moyo zaidi ni kwamba nusu hizi mbili kwa wakati mmoja angalau zinajua kusoma na kuandika na zinafahamiana. Si kuwa ati ni wageni wasiojuana kabisa.

Syllabus
By Rochelle Potkar

At the movie appreciation class, they speak of movies in Mizo,
Sherdukpen, Dakhani,
Kodava, Kosali, Avadhi,
Bishnupriya Manipuri, Uttarakhandi, Maithili,
Santali, Konkani, and Nepali.

Of language racism, and how it shouldn't be.
At the theatre appreciation class, they speak of
sound-and-light synchrony, dialog delivery,
tenor and timbre of body,
stage space, experimentalism,
and *les expressions facials*.

Watch films with your eyes closed
to gauge echoes, breathing, or mute the screen,
submerging one layer to let out the other.

What if simultaneously
they also did a people appreciation program? I think.
Telling us how to look at someone who's not like us,
doesn't speak our language, and is not our friend,
doesn't agree with us, or might never bend
to please us or be of any use to us?

What senses to block? What do we sharpen?
To know his back story or her road less taken?

What lens do we remove? What light to brighten?
To watch her minus her hair, skin, and accent?

Brand of clothing?

Not his order on the table,
but the way he talks to the server.
Not his torn chappals,
but that he never uses a swear word.

What angles do we darken? How do we zoom in?
As he puts his point across politely, at gun point, knife point?

Watch with your eyes closed first,
and listen perhaps to an underlying rhythm
the same subtext - of a hunger for love, acceptance?

I wish someone had told us to substitute sound for light,
light for visual, visual for emotion,
emotion in spectrum, spectrum for empathy,
for touch, for smile,
for soul, for essence
for the same heartbeat
the same beating *dhadkhan, mutuko dhukdhuki,*
dubrai, hrudaya spandana, ridai renag tarko,
lungphu, yada badepa, or kalzachi udi.

Silabasi

Na Rochelle Potkar

Translated into Kiswahili by Kariuki wa Nyamu

Katika ukumbi wa tathmini ya maonyesho, wanazungumza kuhusu
filamu katika Mizo, Sherdukpen, Dakhani, Kodava, Kosali, Avadhi,
Bishnupriya Manipuri, Uttarakhandi, Maithili,
Santali, Konkani na Nepali.
Kuhusu ubaguzi wa rangi wa lugha na vile haifai kuwa.

Katika ukumbi wa tathmini ya maonyesho, wanazungumza kuhusu
upatanisho wa sauti-na-mwangaza, kuwasilisha kwa dayalojia,
daraja za sauti, ubora wa sauti itokayo kwa zana,
nafasi ya steji, majaribio,
na *kiwango cha kutumia viziada lugha.*

Tazama filamu ukifungua macho
upime mwangwi, ukipumua au kupunguza sauti kwa skrini,
ukizamisha safu moja ili nyingine ionekane.

Je, iwapo kwa pamoja
wangewasilisha utaratibu kwa watu? Nawazia tu.
Watueleze namna ya kumchukulia mtu asiyefanana nasi,
asiyezungumza lugha yetu na asiye rafiki yetu,
asiyekubaliana nasi, au ambaye katu hatokubali
kutupendeza au kuwa wa umuhimu wowote kwetu?

Ni hisi zipi zakuzuia? Ni nini cha kutia makali?
Kujua asili yake au aliyoyakosa?

Ni lenzi gani tuondoe? Ni mwangaza upi tuongezee?
Tumtazame pasi nywele yake, ngozi yake na lafudhi yake?

Aina yake ya mavazi?

Si anachoagiza mezani,
Lakini namna anavyomzungumzia mhudumu.
Si sapatu zake tambara,
ila tu hathubutu kutumia neno lolote la kiapo.

Ni pembe zipi tutatia giza? Tutailetaje karibu?
Anaponena kwa upole, kwa bunduki, kwa jisu?

Tazama kwanza kwa macho yaliyofungwa,
Na pengine usikilize midundo ya kimsingi
Masuala ni yale yale– ya njaa ya mapenzi, kukubalika?

Laiti mtu angelituambia tubadili sauti kuwa mwangaza,
mwangaza kuwa kuona, kuona kuwa hisia,
hisia kuwa wigo, wigo uwe uelewa,
uwe kugusa, uwe tabasamu,
uwe nafsi, uwe dhati,
uwe mpigo ule wa moyo,
ukipiga *dhadkhan, mutuko dhukdhuki,*
dubrai, hrudaya, spandana, ridai, renag tarko,
lungphu, yada bapeda, au kalzachi udi.

Art of critiquing
By Rochelle Potkar

An artist once asked me, "What if people do not like my poetry?"
and I said "There are many genres to choose from and
I remember a poetry party where once my poem was shortlisted.
Now this was Hyderabad and we sat circularly
opening our mouths to whiffs of wet spice, an onion rind, and slivers
of spices -
long-grain piano-fingers, and a ballerina's twirls over tongue.
Dum-cooked in earthen pots slow on clay bricks…
and a man beside me says he did not like my poetry."

In those mild winters, in that air-conditioning things began seeping
in.
I looked at his plate, cold on the table.
And said that it was fine. "Don't feel so bad about it."
But he wasn't done yet - he began by telling me which stanzas.
I ate with distaste. [There are different kinds of biryanis cooked all
over India
Saffron-flavored, permutations of rice, spice, herbs, and meat.]

But this man was serious about his critique.

He stood up then and walked over to the other poets.
For some the spices eroded from their plates.
For some their biryanis tasted better."

So I told my student that anyone may not like your work,
And they can send *low-priority* emails
if their thoughts are unsolicited, first evaluating if it will benefit,
and befit an "art of constructive critique" manual,
like tender recipes of biryani.

after getting off notions of self-importance.

Because our tongues are ever-evolving, our taste and hunger too,
but he is free-er not to buy a book that costs just rupees 304.

But he cannot oh, he just cannot
spoil your moment with biryani.

Sanaa ya uchambuzi
Na Rochelle Potkar
Translated into Kiswahili by Kariuki wa Nyamu

Msanii mmoja aliwahi niuliza, "Je, iwapo ikiwa watu hawapendi ushairi wangu?"
nami nikamjibu "Kuna tanzu nyingi za kuchagua na
nakumbuka sherehe moja ya ushairi pale shairi langu lilichaguliwa.
Huku kulikuwa Hyderabad ambapo tuliketi mduara
tukifungua vinywa vyetu kwa harufu ya viungo vilivyoloa, ganda la
kitunguu, cheche za viungo-
punje ndefu kama vidole vya piano, na mzunguko wa maigizo kwenye
ulimi.
Vyote vimepikwa ndani ya vyungu kwenye matofali ya kuokwa...
na mtu aliye karibu nami anasema hakupenda ushairi wangu."

Wakati ule baridi ikipungua, katika hali hiyo ya hewa mambo yalianza
taratibu.
Nikaangalia sahani yake, ikiwa baridi hapo mezani.
Na nikasema yote ni shwari. "Usihisi vibaya kunihusu."
Lakini hakuwa amemaliza- akaanza kuniambia ni beti zipi
Nikavumilia. [Kuna biriani aina nyingi zinazoandaliwa kote India
Yenye ladha ya zafarani, wali aina mbali mbali, viungo, mboga za
kienyeji, na nyama.]

Walakini huyu mtu alikuwa anamaanisha katika uchambuzi wake.

Kisha akasimama na kuelekea kwa malenga wengine
Kwa wengine, viungo vilizidi katika sahani zao.
Kwa wengine, biriani zao zilionja ladha zuri."

Hivyo nikamwambia mwanafunzi wangu ya kwamba kuna wale
hawatapenda kazi yako ya usanii,

Na wanaweza tuma barua pepe za kuvunja moyo
iwapo fikra zao hazijaitishwa, kuikagua kama itawanufaisha
na kuorodheshwa kama mwongozo wa "sanaa ya uchambuzi wa
kiwango cha juu"
kama resipe nyororo za biriani
baada ya kupuuza fikira za kujivuna.

Kwa sababu ndimi zetu zaendelea kubadilika, vilevile ladha yetu na
njaa pia,
lakini ako huru kutonunua kitabu cha rupia 304.

Lakini katu hawezi, hawezi kamwe
haribu wakati wako na biriani.

BURRIED SECRECT
By Juma Brenda

The strong men of the village had to do it,
Three strong ropes passing under to ease the work,
As it went down slowly by slowly, I knew it was FINISHED,
The three ropes symbolized something,
The three stages of life.
A Sharp tear dropped and fell direct to his head,
According to our culture,
"IT IS A BAD OMEN" the elders said.
It didn`t bother me much, he gave me life, I had to.
It was pricking painful.
With My hands shaking, took the soil on my palm,
Threw it inside and said bye!
After a week everyone had gone,
We remained alone,
My mum, two brothers and I,
And it dawned, we don't have him anymore. Tough life commenced.

"Min Atieno you can't continue like this, you need a man," one said.
"I can make the best husband, just like the late," another suggested.
"According to our culture, you must be remarried," another insisted.
"She has to be remarried immediately, remember she has two boys,
 Oloo you're the one, because the late was your immediate follower"
the elders confirmed.

Seeing him match as a warrior into our house shook me,
And I, immediately knew it was FINISHED.
How?
Together we were the cause of my dad's death,
How?
'Chira'

He took advantage of my innocence,
And here I am carrying my 'father's child',
My mother's second husband.
No!
Like the elders said 'IT IS A BAD OMEN'
It is FINISHED.
No one would ever know,
Buried secret.

*Chira- taboo in the African society
*min atieno – mother to Atieno

Sumasɛm

Juma Brenda anwonsɛm
Translated into Akan Twi by Adjei Agyei-Baah

Mmarantiea naɛwɔkuro no mu naɛwɔsɛɔdisaaadwuma no
naehianhomammieɛnsanaɔdeadisaaadwuma no
naberɛ a ɔdenhoma no faaaseɛnkakrakakra no, namenimsɛbibiara aba awieyɛ
nanhomammieɛnsa no gyinahɔ ma biribi
abrabɔmponponsoɔmmieɛnsa
nisuopueprɛkopɛnaɛtɔɔ ne tiri so
nayɛnamamerɛ mu no
naɛyɛakyiwade

Na anha me pii, naɔnonaɔmaa me nkwa, entinaewɔsɛ meyɔ
Na naɛyɛyapii
Mede me nsa a ɛrepofaanɔtefiri me nsayam
to baa mu na me kaasɛbaabaae
Na ne nawɔtwe mu a obiarakɔeɛ
ɛkayɛnkoara
Me maame, me nuanommmarimammienu ne me
Na ɛpusuyɛnsɛyahwere no. Abrabɔ mu hyɛɛaseɛyɛɛ den

"Atienomaamewontumintena no seiara, wo bɛhiabarima",
ɔbaakopaamukae.
"Metumiayɛkunupatesɛwo kunu awoafiri mu no,
ɔfoforɔkyerɛɛn'adwene
Sɛneayɛnamamerɛkyerɛno, ɛsɛsɛwoware bio, ɔfoforɔnso de too so
ɛwɔsɛɔwaremprenprenara, ɛfirisɛɔwɔmarimmammienu
Oloo, wone nipa wosina nan a ɛyɛyie, efirisɛɔwufoɔyɛ wo nuaketewa,
mpanimfoɔ no siiso dua.

Na mehwɛsɛɔtutuu ne nan sɛɔkofoɔ baa yɛnfiepusuu me

253

Na mehunuusɛbibiara aba awieɛ
Kwan bɛn so?
Efirisɛyɛnmmienunaɛkabomkumyɛn papa
Ɛkwanbɛn so?
"Kyira"
Ɔde ne nyansabuu me kwasea
Ɛnesɛmegyina hayikutam'agyabayi,
Me maamekunu a ɔtɔso mmienu
Daabi!
Sɛneampaninsieɛ "ɛyɛakyiwadeɛ"
Bibiara aba awieɛ,
Obiaraasonnhunu
Ahintasɛm!

*Kyira- taboo in the African society
*Atienomaame -mother of Atieno

A Dirge for the Delta

By Stephen Temitope David

Come to me dear song
Come to me like the forgotten winds
Blowing along abandoned shores, unearthing hidden shells of venal feasts
Come to me like the incessant pestering of the mosquitoes' lullaby
Taunting poisoned nets
And shaved heads.

Come to me like the painful, yet absent memory of yesterday's dream
A postmodern pot of confusing spices
Making me lost in a maze of many me
A hollow maze where mothers' cries rend the air like the old garments on our backs
While children turn deaf ears to warning shots

Come to me like the pungent smell of the fisherman's abandoned canoe
Along the oil complex
With sights baptised with fires and bullets of brotherly guards
Bought with bloody dollars
Loaded guns and foreign gins
Enjoying lazy nights in familiar battle fronts
They drink from the fiery beaded waists of anxious girls

Come to me
Oh come to me like a touch of hot coals
Like a stomach devouring its hungry self in hunger
Like the painful joy of abandoned carcasses
happy meals for a party of vultures
Like the happy dirge they will sing at her funeral

At the death of earth
When her blood is emptied in barrels of greed!

Benabɔ Nwom MaDɛlta

Stephen Temitope David anwonsɛm

Translated into Akan Twi by Adjei Agyei Baah

Bra me nkyɛn mawerhoɔdwom
Bra me nkyɛn sɛhwimhwimmframa
A renammpoanoa obiarannihɔ
narebuebuesunamkwankoraɛhyehyɛ nɔteɛmu
Bra me nkyɛn sɛntontom a ɔrentegyae,
naɔpesɛɔbɛsintomaw'ahyɛ no aduro so
Na w'asaneasitirikwakwaeɛ so

Bra me nkyɛn sɛ yaw aɛnnianisoɔdeaduro
Mprenprengyinaberɛa nteasennyɛadwuma
Na ma menyera wɔ me nhunumuu mu
Kɔpemmpɛnpɛnsoɔ a nanomsudensunsuan
ntomadadaaguuyɛn akyi
berɛ a mmɔfrabu wɔn asomnnua wɔɔyone a ɛrebaho

Bra me nkyɛn sɛmframabɔne a firimpataayifoɔkodoɔa woagya no wɔ
baabi a wɔtufamnwo
Anisoɔ a ɛredɛre gyaɛfirianuanoma ɔbɔ wɔnhowɔho ban
firimogyahuegu sika ne amanonensaden
Wɔbereɔregye wɔn anianadowwɔnkwankwaanuase
na wɔnani di akyini wɔmaayiwaahweneɛ so

Bra me kyɛn
O bra me nkyɛn sɛegyafruma a ɛgukoropɔto mu
Sɛ yɛfunu a ɛrewe ne ho wɔ ne kɔm muo
Tesɛakɔkɔsɛkyi a ɔrebɔse wɔnamfunu soɔ
Tesɛanigyeɛawerɛhoɔdwom a wɔn bɛto wɔnayiease
Wɔberɛ a asaase bɛwu
kɔsi sɛ ne mogya a adufrupɛahyɛmuma bɛsa

257

A Song for Independence
By Stephen Temitope David

Dance in my head
Oh sweet song of freedom
Emerge like Madiba's gait through those sucking gates
From drowning trips down lanes of hate
That entombs in nameless lands of cursed smiles in rampart spate.

Dance in my throat oh sweet song
Songs like the awoko chirrups at the sight of the fowler
Blinded by the winter sun
Stumbles into snares set for bellicose preys.

Possess my feet oh sweet song
Whistled along farm paths
In years when innocence was a blessing still
And success peeped from the pages of printed leaves
Cocoa, groundnuts and oil palm in the grasps of new leaders.

Twist my innards not oh sweet song
I sing of new hands to plough the same field
Yielding a new harvest of rich tears
Our yams rotten in weed betrothed fields
In the midst of new found gold,
We plough rich bloods
From old lands in new anguish
A new dirge for the celebration emerges,
No new song for the torn pages of our history
Like the fractured hands of a votary to pitiless gods
We with mucous gaze await the promised change.

Faahodie Nwom
Stephen Temitope anwonsɛm
Translated into Akan Twi by Adjei Agyei Baah

Di asa wɔ me tiri mu
O faahodienwom dɛɛdɛ
Bra tesɛ Madiba nanteɛ a ɔde bɔwuraabofonopono mu
de tuuɔtan ne nnyinyimuso sa
de siesere a nannsekanɛdiakyire

Di ahim wɔ me menemu o nwom dɛɛdɛ
Nnwomtesɛawoko wɔberɛ a woahunufidisumfoɔ
Berɛ a onwunuowiaafiran'ani
naosunti kɔtɔafidie awasum amanwuramakokɔ

ma wo nwom dɛɛdɛntonkye me nansɛgyaman
mbɔ wɔberɛ a m'asiafuomukwan so
Wɔberɛbi anabunuyɛɛyɛnhyira
Na mpuntuopuefirinwoma a woatintim mu
Na kookoo,nkateɛ ne abɛnwokuraakannifonsampampee

Nkyinkyim me munneɛma o nwom dɛɛdɛ
Meto ma afoforɔ a ɔbɛfuntumasaasekorɔyiani
namebotoomaaɔtwaberɛ a ɛmaameteenisuo
na yɛn mmayerɛporɔɔ wɔnfuyɛ mu bɛdane
sɛsikakɔkoɔ a ɔbaako adɔakɔto
na yɛafuntummogyaahwieagunsaasedadaa wɔ abufuhyew so
nadwomfoforɔ yɛde di ahurusie bɛpue
nyɛdwom a yɛde bɛgyeabakwassɛm atɔapiabaaba
tesɛɔsomfonsa a abuo a ɔredesom bosom atirimuɔdenfoɔ
de animu a hwenorɔahyɛ no ma a ɛde nsesayɛreba

Silent Gods (For the kidnapped schoolgirls)
By Stephen Temitope David

Let the muse flowing from the loins of sango blast through me!
Let ogun's drunken fury wielding
a bloodied sword of painless vengeance paint my view.
Let our muffled cries, blackened by the tree of forgetfulness break
the ice!
We are the girls laden with pregnancies of neglect and division
I hear they even dispute our existence and the eerie night of our
limelight
the anguish of marked faces of dried tears
and feasts at our living wake-keeps.

We are the girls at the mercy of his turbaned head
bobbing from doped evenings,
rifles punctuating our sleeping wake.
Thus it has been since our plucked experience.
Blackened heart and teeth flashing at the allure of our luscious waists,
we scream! We prayed to lost gods in denial!

They played and mocked the silent gods with recalcitrant moans of
stolen pleasures.
Our tears birth a river in Sambisa!
We hear the oracle has changed votaries
and the rifle has changed ends.
Indeed the gods are but angry yet
daily we pray to a black tunnel with shadows of a black flag
you know our faces but not our pains,
our town but not our prisons.
Yet we hope the gods remember our gaolers.

Abosom Mmum

Stephen Temitope David anwonsɛm

Translated into Akan Twi by Adjei Agyei Baah

Ma ahotɛw a ɛfirisangoserɛmɛnbɔmfamemu
Na ma mahofamanyɛtesɛogun a wɔaborokutankrantɛnufanu
Ma yɛnnne a awerɛfie ne sumatɔsowerɛembubufasuo
Yɛyɛmmayiwa a yɛnnyinsɛnamayatoyɛnasawram
Na mate sɛebikyerɛsɛyɛnnnihɔ
Anadwoateetee a yɛkɔɔ mu, yaw a ɛmayɛnanisuosaeɛ
Ne apɛsiri a yɛsiiɛ

Yɛyɛmmayiwayɛnabotowɔ ne dukuhuhuuhuanim
a esumahyɛ mu ma,
ne neteabɔɔfrɛɛrediakɔneabawɔnyɛnnna mu
saaara ne yɛtebeafiri da a wɔnhwimyɛnfiri fie
Akoma a aprim ne se a ahyɛnaɛdiyɛnsisi ho fɛw
Yɛ teamu, sane bɔɔmpaeɛkyerɛɛabosom a wɔn apo yɛn

Wɔgyeewɔnani, sane dii abosomɔrengyeyɛn so no ho fɛw
wɔberɛ a ɔrefayɛn
Na yɛnanisuoteneesɛ Sambisa tadeɛ!
Na yɛteesɛɔbosom no asesanaakomfoɔ
Na etuo ne nsaɛdiasesa
Ampanaabosom no boafu
nadabiaranayɛbɔmpaeɛguamenadonkodonko
a nafrankaanniahimwɔ tire
Na na obi bɛhunuyɛnanim, nannyɛyɛn yaw
yɛnnkuro, nannyɛyɛnafiase
Na nayɛwɔgyedieɛsɛyɛnabosombɛkaewɔn a ɔdeyɛnguafiase

The Shape of the Heart
By Ryan Thorpe

is supposed to be the size of
a hand covering a fist, two hands
pumping for a lifetime. Cartoons show
the heart as rounded circles meeting and
tapering off like a memory, the top
peeking out like an ass from sagging
jeans. I imagine the heart as unique,
a ugly smudged fingerprint, as
surprising its owner with each beat;
the valves looking faintly like tip
of a distant lover's nose.

Umbo la Roho

Na Ryan Thorpe

Translated into Kiswahili by Kariuki wa Nyamu

Inafaa kuwa na ukubwa wa
mkono uliokunja ngumi, mikono miwili
inayodunda uhaini wote. Vibonzo huonyesha
roho kama miviringo inayozunguka na kukutana
na kuchangoka kama kumbukizi, juu
ikivutia kama tako katika suruali iliyolegea
nawazia moyo kuwa na upekee,
usiovutia wenye alama chafu za vidole, kama
washangaza mwenyewe na kila mdundo;
mishipa ikionekana dhaifu kama ncha
ya pua la mpenzi wa nchi za mbali.

Walking to Work in Shanghai
By Ryan Thorpe

Each day I select a different path
to work—small changes in my arbitrary
existence—derivations from an established
pheromone track—today I see a trash man
scrubbing the Dumpster wearing pink waders
with his head wrapped in a red bandana—
he hums and sings as he sprays the
water, arcing it to remove the grime, scraping
the rust-red water with a rubber blade.

Yesterday I watched a girl walking six dogs—
they pulled her through streets like a sled—
she clung to a stoplight, strangling the dogs
off the road. She smiled as I passed.

Tomorrow I will walk through the clothing market,
hoping to watch sellers push shirts onto
high poles with bamboo sticks, and I will glance
at others counting footsteps toward the usual
subway, passing the the drunk who waves his
hands as batons as if he conducted the world.

Kutembea hadi Kazini Jijini Shanghai

Na Ryan Thorpe
Translated into Kiswahili by Kariuki wa Nyamu

Kila siku nachagua njia tofauti
kwenda kazini– mabadiliko machache katika uamuzi wa
uwepo wangu– ninaufikia kutoka nafsini
mwangu– leo naona mtupa taka
akisugua pipa la taka akivalia gambuti za rangi ya waridi
mikono yake kaifunga na kijitambaa chekundu–
yeye huvuma huku akinyunyizia
maji, akiyalenga ndani kutoa masazo, akiondosha
maji mekundu yenye kutu kwa kafi ya mpira.

Jana nilitazama binti akitembeza mbwa sita
walimvuta mitaani kama kijigari cha kuvutiwa barafuni
alijishikilia kwenye mlingoti wa taa za trafiki, akiwanyonga mbwa hao
kando ya barabara. Alitabasamu nilipokuwa nikipita.

Kesho nitatembea katikati ya soko la nguo,
nikitumaini nitawaona wauzaji wakipandisha mashati kwenye
milingoti mirefu kwa kutumia miti mianzi, na nitatupia macho
wengine watakaokuwa wakizambua nyayo kuelekea vijiani
huku nikipita mlevi anayepunga mikono yake
kama rungu kana kwamba anaelekezwa na ulimwengu.

(untitled)
By Daniel Ari

Add salt to water and stir, no
add oil to water and agitate with a nuclear-powered blender until:
they agree with each other
they are homogeneous molecularly
they do not separate on salads, on issues or on cross-town busses

Add salt and stir. Add ash and stir. Add a tiny bit of poison.
Poison never hurt anybody. Trace amounts. Balance the accounts.

Zoom in on the thought behind
the decision to purchase a nuclear-powered blender.

(untitled)

Daniel Ari

Translation into Japanese by Fumio Ueno

水に塩を入れて混ぜる。いいえ、

水に油を入れて、原子力ミキサーでかき混ぜる。分量は…

お互いが納得できるまで。

分子的に同質になるまで。

サラダの中で、問題の上で、町を走るバスの中で、ばら
ばらでなくなるまで。

塩を入れて混ぜる。灰を加えて混ぜる。ほんの少し毒を入れ
て。

毒は決して誰も傷つけない。ほんの少し。分量を調節して。

原子力ミキサーを買おうと決めるときの思いに深く焦点をあ
てて。

Benjamina Tree
By Shannon Hopkins

The afternoon light sits pooled
in the spoons of the leaves,
so alive, this tree.
It has grown broad
off the fat, loamy earth –
its roots reaching
from a pivot-rod,
and drawn back in again
by the pulse in the soil.
The leaves,
wedges crisp as ice,
exude such wellness.
Stupefied and slow
with the sun
it grows not at all
until one afternoon
it is taller than I.

Benjamina Tree

By Shannon Hopkins

Translation into Japanese by Fumio Ueno

午後の光が葉っぱのスプーンの上にじっと溜まる

活き活きしている、この木。

大きく育っている。脂肪分がなく、ローム質の土壌で－

その根は旋回する枝から届いて、土壌の脈拍によってまた引き戻される。

この木は、氷のようにしゃっとしたくさび形で、

健康なさまを滲み出す。

日の光とともにゆっくりぼうっとたたずんで、

午後までに木は全く成長していない。

私より背が高かったんだね。

Freedom?
By Shannon Hopkins

I wanted milk
But it was after dark…
I needed fuel for my car
But it was the bad part of town…
- my movements decided by a

Kangaroo curfew.
So I just drink black coffee.
Drive on in the red.
(Must remember to lock the gate)
So then where is this
Freedom
We fought for?
So many died for.
We are still dying.
I have seen a man hang himself
for lack of money to keep body and soul
I have seen the drying mauve blood
- Smeared like an artist's failed canvas –

of a man
shot in taxi war crossfire
he was on his way home
from an honest day.
I have seen a man so crazed
with it all
he ran naked on Durban's busiest highway.
My eyes still burn.
I have read of young women
raped and disemboweled

by friends.
Left where they lay.
I have read of things done
to children and old people
that I cannot make myself write.
The people are still angry.
They tear at each other with long, uneasy claws.
Where is this freedom we fought for then?
Still hungry
clinging to the shadows
looking for a cause.
Still quivering in the whispered promises
and promises
and promises
that grow stale
become dust
and are carried away
on the hot afternoon winds.

We are here
By Shannon Hopkins

Yes, we are here.
We are not at home
but we are not not at home.
The African earth is soaked with the umbilical blood
of a thousand nations.
Some of our fathers
sweated also to unlock the chains
of our African brothers and sisters
and together we throw away,
no longer possess
the fetters.
By our very birth
our green ID cards
we are Africans.
Yes, we are here.
And yes, we are one.

Hair things
By Tralone Lindiwe Khoza

My face is red like the sun, beaded in truth by colours all around me...
The crisp of the wind woes me. My hair has a mind of its own
I sift through it, to mine for gold found in Johannesburg
I came, I stood and I listened to
the voice of the rainbow,
The dreams of my grandmother hidden inside the sarong with the
Shangaan colours.
I want to speak, but the words won't come
I long to sing, my lungs are rested
I want to cheer, the cymbal is too far, I, want to cheer
because my face is red like the sun beaded in truth by colours all
around me.

God I want to go to Ghana
By Tralone Lindiwe Khoza

So my soul can believe that close friends Burkino Faso and Ivory Coast are near

I want to taste the West African air with my very own nostrils

I want to thank the land for raising warrior Kings- Ghana is your name

I want to touch the soil that is close to the hue of my skin

I want to hold the womb of Gold and cocoa

I want to embrace women for wearing headscarves and flowing tapestries of deep and bright coloured African fabrics of the rainbow.

I want to remember how women carried buckets of water on the heads and now can they run thriving businesses.

I want to see Kofi Annan's home and where Eric Kodjoe who begot Boris came from

I want to go to Ghana and see the beauty of my people, the Akan Ashanti people

And be welcomed – Akwaaba!

I want to fall in love with what Maya Angelou saw.

I want to feel alive and be covered in multicoloured beads of the stories of the nation

God I really want to go to Ghana.

Plays

Lonely Bites.
A short play by Albert Jamae

SYNOPSIS
A little girl's hunger for friendship takes her to the darkest of places.
CHARACTERS
ANNIE (9) – little spritely girl, think orphan Annie
OLD MAN (60+) – tall, pale, sullen face and sickly
SETTING
Suburban house (kitchen).

INT. OLD HOUSE/KITCHEN - NIGHT
A dirty kitchen as if no-one has lived there for a year. The decor would hint at an old lady's abode and dimly lit. A table and two chairs. Some dirty dishes on the bench, a knife block full of knives, a fancy teapot and cups.

ANNIE (9), dressed in dirty and battered clothes, enters from outside, panicked and out of breath. She shuts the door hard behind her, then peeks carefully through the window.
She quickly reels back as if being spotted.

She has another look out the window to check the coast is clear, and appears relieved. She turns back to see the room around her and scrunches her face in disapproval.
She runs her finger in the dust of the window sill and playfully hums. (The nursery rhyme 'there was an old woman who ate a fly'.)
CREAK. *She turns in fright at the noisy floorboards.*
OLD MAN *hovers in the darkened corner on the opposite side of the kitchen.*
ANNIE: Hello?
She anxiously steps closer.
ANNIE: I know you're there. I saw you peeking through the window when I was dealing with those pesky boys.
No response.

ANNIE: They've gone now so you can come out if you like.

Still nothing.

ANNIE: Helloooooo?!

She innocently waves into the darkness, then stops with a new thought.

ANNIE: Did Mrs Edgley go on holidays? Because I haven't seen her for ages! Do you know when she'll be back?

She waits for a response but nothing. She gives up and plonks herself on the kitchen chair by the table, playfully humming again. She stops with a sudden thought.

ANNIE: Are you her new boyfriend? I don't remember her saying she had a boyfriend. But she did tell me about this nice man Reggie who would come and cut her lawns for her...ohhh...you must be Reggie!

She gets up and curtseys.

ANNIE: Pleased to meet you Reggie! I'm Annie.

She takes another step closer.

ANNIE: (stage whisper) It's looking like a jungle out there Reggie! You might want to cut the grass soon, before Mrs Edgley comes back, or she'll get cross with you!

Still no response so she deflates.

ANNIE: Alright. Maybe you want to be alone. I can go if you want me to.

She sighs and turns to look out the window.

ANNIE: I just hope those boys don't come back.

She rubs her arm.

ANNIE: The rocks really hurt me this time.

She turns to face him.

ANNIE: The bruise is still there from last week when they hit me with a stick. See?!

She overtly shows her neck.

ANNIE: I think a vein might be popping out!

He shuffles anxiously in the shadows.

She puffs out defeated and turns back to the door.

277

ANNIE: Okay Reggie. I'm going.

She shuffles slowly — hoping he'll notice her. Playing up with a bigger 'sigh'. It's not working. She stops defiantly and preens herself.

ANNIE: Actually Sir Reginald, I think you're right. It would be rude of me if I didn't stay for a spot of tea. I'm sure you could use the company.

She turns to glare at him defiantly.

ANNIE: Especially if Mrs Edgley is away.

Pause.

ANNIE: I'm not leaving until we have our tea Reggie.

He reluctantly shuffles out from the shadows balancing on a cane. His face very pale, his eyes bloodshot and he looks like death warmed up. He coughs, trying to suppress his ill health.

She wipes the chair clean with her clothes and signals for him to sit.

He reluctantly sits.

She suddenly beams a big smile.

ANNIE: Wonderful. It's a bit dark in here. I'll just turn the light on.

He flinches.

She tries a switch but it doesn't work. She flicks it on and off a dozen times to make sure.

ANNIE: You really must change these light bulbs. Mrs Edgley never liked a dark kitchen. Oh well, it'll have to be a tea party by candlelight.

She rummages through the drawers and finds a candle and matches. She takes them to the table and lights it. She uses a lot of matches to get it lit.

ANNIE: Mrs Edgley said it's okay for me to use matches now because I watched her do it so many times.

The candle is finally lit.

ANNIE: There we go. Now…tea.

She looks around the kitchen bench and finds a dusty tea pot and cups, blowing the dust off and coughing at it.

She stands at the sink, reaching up holding the tea pot. She turns the tap on but no water comes out. She sighs, shrugs her shoulders and pretends its filling up the pot. She hums her nursery rhyme while she waits.

ANNIE: Yep that should be enough.

She turns off the tap and carries the tray to the table. She pours the pretend tea into two dusty cups, still humming, then pours the pretend milk.

ANNIE: Now it's not tea without milk and sugar.

She pops in pretend sugar and stirs each cup a dozen times. Then she waits. He waits and she rolls her eyes.

ANNIE: (condescending) It's ready.

He cautiously takes the cup as she sips hers delicately.

ANNIE: How has your day been Reggie?

He just looks at her and she doesn't wait for an answer.

ANNIE: I visited Mrs Griffiths this evening, just around the corner. I wish you could've been there, she was so sweet. We had tea and crackers and she would talk so nicely - except when she got cross at me for spilling crumbs on her couch. Then I got cross, then she got crosser, then I...but it all worked out fine.

She notices he hasn't touched his tea and clears her throat indignantly, motioning for him to drink.

He obliges with a small sip.

ANNIE: You would've liked her. She's lonely...and old, just like you.

He's put in his place.

ANNIE: Then on my way back those silly boys started teasing me again. Just because I wear the same clothes every day doesn't mean I'm a dirty rat! They called me other things too which I'm not going to tell you because Mrs Edgley would say 'nobody likes a little girl who says those words!'

She sips her tea and then studies his face.

ANNIE: You could smile a bit more Reggie. Here, I'll show you.

She puts her cup down and beams a big toothy smile.

ANNIE: (through gritted teeth) See? Now your turn.

He has no intention of smiling and glares at her.

She sighs, disappointed and continues studying his face.
ANNIE: Hmmm. You're hungry aren't you?
He shifts awkwardly.
ANNIE: You look like you haven't eaten for a very long time.
She keeps looking at him.
ANNIE: I know what you need.
He looks hopeful.
ANNIE: Cake!
He deflates.
She hops up and looks around the bench – nothing. Sees an empty plate and her eyes light up. She ceremoniously brings the plate to the table.
ANNIE: Doesn't this look lovely!
She places the empty plate on the table between them.
He looks at it bemused.
ANNIE: I know Reggie - it's not cut up yet. Mrs Edgley still says I'm too little to use knives so you'll have to do it.
She motions for him to move and he slowly makes his way to the kitchen. He spots the grubby knife block, pulls out the largest knife and the blade is still shiny. He pauses in thought.
She sits at the table swinging her legs, waiting, humming her nursery rhyme.
He returns slowly. Places the knife on the table beside the plate and sits; exhausted from the walk. He uses his cane to push the knife towards her.
Her eyes widen with wonder.
ANNIE: Really?!
She carefully takes the knife and looks at it admiringly.
ANNIE: You see, the maids don't let me have cake very often. I don't know why. Maybe because when I start eating it I can't...
She notices his tea cup is still on the table and frowns.
ANNIE: If you don't drink your tea you'll get thirsty. And if you're too thirsty you'll get sick. And if you get sick you might die. And if you die...you can't have any cake.
His mouth crinkles with intolerance as he breathes deeper through his nose.
ANNIE: You don't want to die do you?

280

She gestures with the knife for him to pick up the cup.

He slowly brings the cup to his lips and sips the pretend tea.

ANNIE: Good. Now you can have cake.

She proceeds to cut the pretend cake. He watches her carefully with the knife.

ANNIE: You've done such a lovely job with this Sir Reginald. The texture is simply marvellous. I must get the recipe from you so I can...

Her hand slips and she cuts herself; wincing in pain.

His heart stops a beat; his breath quickens.

Blood trickles from her finger and he watches, mesmerised.

ANNIE: Oh no. She was right. I am too young to use a knife!

He starts to tremble in anxiety. The cup and saucer clinking in his shaky hands.

Annie sucks her finger and notices his reaction.

ANNIE: What's wrong? It's just blood. See?

She holds up her bloody finger to show him; it continues to trickle.

He begins to hyperventilate and drops the cup on the floor. It smashes. His heart rate intensifies as does his coughing as he struggles to breathe.

She gawks in shock at the broken cup.

ANNIE: Well that wasn't very nice was it?! Mrs Edgley would get very angry if she saw you broke her special china!

He glares at her and growls angrily.

She mimics his growl in return – refusing to be intimidated.

She hops off the chair and stomps towards the window, huffing.

A few moments before they begin to calm down.

ANNIE: I'm sorry Reggie. I don't like getting cross. Sometimes it means I end up alone. It's not much fun is it?

She turns to look at him.

ANNIE: Being lonely.

He looks away.

She sucks her finger clean and looks at it sadly.

ANNIE: I know you don't want tea, or cake. But I think it helps - if we're going to be friends. You do want to be friends don't you Reggie?

She glances at him discreetly but he doesn't budge.

She gazes out the window.

ANNIE: Mrs Edgley was my friend, for a long time. But I don't think I'll be seeing her again will I?

She throws him a knowing look.

He turns away guiltily.

She turns back, solemnly doodling on the window with her finger.

ANNIE: That's okay Reggie. I'm used to it.

He slowly rises out of the chair, using all his strength to stand.

ANNIE: If you want me to leave just say so and I'll...

OLD MAN: Nikolai.

She turns back and gasps quietly in surprise to see him standing nobly before her.

OLD MAN: My name. Nikolai.

Her face lights up with elation, then proceeds with a ladylike curtsy.

ANNIE: An honour to meet you, Sir Nikolai.

Their warm moment disrupted by Annie turning to notice something through the window.

ANNIE: Oh no. They're back.

Her worry quickly turns into a new thought.

ANNIE: Now that we're friends, we have to do everything together! So you just wait there, I'll be right back.

She heads for the door.

He motions concern for her — he clearly doesn't want her to go out.

She turns back coyly.

ANNIE: Oh Nikolai I'll be fine. I just want to invite them in for tea. There's plenty to go around.

She smiles and races out the door.

He's a little perplexed and places his walking cane on the table.

ANNIE: (off stage) Hey fat heads! I dare you to come in and get me! Unless you're just a couple of scared little girls!

His eyes sparkle with a new lease of life. He starts breathing deeply with a mix of anticipation and satisfaction.

ANNIE: (off stage to Nikolai) Here they come!

She re-enters, backing away from the door.

ANNIE: I'm so glad we found each other Nikolai.

She holds his hand.

ANNIE: You're the first real friend I've had in a hundred years.

She looks up at him with affection.

They share a smile - he has visible fangs.

So does she.

She blows out the candle and LIGHTS fade on them waiting as she playfully hums her nursery rhyme.

*****

Cizo Daya tilo

Gajeruwar wasa daga Albert Jamae

Translation into Hausa by Abdulrahman S. Waziri and Mustapha Tanko

KADDAMARWA

Bukatar kawaye yakai karamar yarinya mammunan wurare.

YAN WASA

ANNIE (9) - marainiya Annie, karamar yarinya yar baiwa

TSOHO (60+) – dogo, mai haske,cikekken fuska kuma rago

SHIRI

Gidan Suburban (madafi)

TSOHUWAR GIDA/MADAFI-DARE

Kaza miyar madafi kamar ba'a amfani dashi har tsawon shekara.
Kayan ado zai dishe hasken gidan tsohuwan. Tebur da kujeru biyu.
Wadan su dattin tasa akan benci,
Wuka makil a kube, tukunyan shayi na kawa da kofuna.
ANNIE (9),sanye da dattin yageggen kaya, ta shigo a gigice ta rufe kofa da karfi sai ta leki taga.
Ta jabaya cikin hanzari tamkar an ganta.
Ta sake leka tagan domin duban ko hadari ta wase,daalamu ba masala.
Ta juya baya ta kalli cikin dakin ta bata fuska.
Ta sanya yatsar ta a kura dake dankare a taga tana wasa dashi (wakar yara 'akwai wata tsohuwa tana cin kuda)
CREAK. Tajuya a tsorace akan dabe.

TSOHO labe a wata kusurwa mai duhu gaban madafi.

ANNIE: Sannu?

Cikin juyayi ta maso kusa.

ANNIE: nasan kana nan. Na hangekada na leka taga lokacinkana fama da sakararrun samarukan nan.

Ba amsa

ANNIE:sun tafi zaka iya fitowa in kana bukata.

Haryanzu shiru.

ANNIE: sannuuuuu?

Ta doshi duhun ta tsayatayi wata tunani.

ANNIE: Shin Mrs Edgley taje hutu ne? domin banganta ba na tsawon lokaci! Ko ka san

Lokacin da zata dawo?

Ta saurari amsa amma shiru. Ta hakura sai ta dubi kujera kusa da tebur a madafi tayi zamanta, a shashance. Wata tunani yafado mata.

ANNIE: Kaine sabon saurayin tane? Bana tunanin idan ta tabace tana da saurayi.

Amma ta bani labarin mutumin kirki Reggie wanda ke zuwa ya rage ciyawa…

Kaine Raggie!

Ta mike ta marabce shi

ANNIE: nayi farin cikin saduwa da Raggie! Nice Annie

Ta maso kusa.

ANNIE: (rada a bayan fage)can yayi kamar kurmi Raggie! Zaka so ka tsare ciyawan nan bada jumawa ba

Kafin Mrs Edgley ta dawo,ko zata bata rai!

Haryanzu ba amsa sai ta hakura.

ANNIE: shi kenan,kana son ka kadaita ne. zan tafi idan kana bukatan haka.

Tajuya ta dubi taga.

ANNIE: inna fatan kara samarukan nan su dawo.

Ta shafa hanun ta.

ANNIE: wadarin nan yayi mini zafi wannan karon.

Tajuya ta fiskance shi.

ANNIE: rauni da suka yi mini saka makon bugu na da sanda da sukayimakon daya wuce bai warke ba. Gani?

Ta bude wuyar tata nuna.

ANNIE: Inna tunanin kamar hanyar jinni ya fito!

cikin jayayiyabi inuwa.

Ta numfasa a kasala ta juya ta fiskan ci kofa.

ANNIE: shikenanRaggie. Zan tafi.

Tayi tattaki sannu a hankali-da fatan zai gano ta. Tana waswasi.

Baiya aiki. Ta saurara da takama

ANNIE: kwarai Ranka ya dade Reginald, inna ganin kayi gaskiya. Zai zama rashin hankali idan ban tsaya na sha shayi ba. Na tabbata zaka amfana da kasance wana.

Ta waiwaye shi da murmushi.

ANNIE:musamman idan ba Mrs Edgley.

Saurara

ANNIE: badan tafi ba sai munsha shayi Raggie.

Ya masa daga inuwar sa ya dogara da kokara. Fiskar sa a daure, idonsa sunyi ja tamkar

Wanda ke halin rai kwawai mutu kwakwai. Yayi tari domin rage radadin rashin lafiya.

Ta share kujera sap da kayan ta sannan tayi masa alama ya zauna.

Ya zauna.

Sai tayi doguwar murmushi.

ANNIE: abin mamaki akwai duhu anan,zan kunna wuta.

Ya ja baya.

Ta gwada amma makunni baya aiki. Tayi da dama baiyi ba.

ANNIE: dole ne a sake kwayayen wutan nan. Mrs Edgley bata son madafi mai duhu.

Shike nan damuyi bukin shan shayin da hasken kendir.

Ta duba cikin durowan tebur ta samu kendir da ashana ta kaisu kan tebur ta kunna.

bayanyunkuri da dama.

ANNIE: Mrs Edgley ta amince nayi amfani da ashana saboda nasha lura da ita wurin amfani dashi.

Akarshe kendir ya kama.

ANNIE: mai ya rage yanzu…shayi.

Ta duba kan bencin madafi taga tukunyan shayi da kofuna masu kura,ta fure su

Hakan ya sata tari.

Taje mawanki da tukunyan shayin. Ta bude fanfo amma ba ruwa.

Ta kada kafadan ta tamkar ruwan na zuba tana reraye-reraye

ANNIE: Hakika yayi

Ta rufe fanfo sai ta dauki tire zuwa kan tebur. Ta zuba shayin riyar ta a kofuna masu kuran sannan ta zuba madara.

ANNIE: ba shayi bane idan ba madara da sukari.

Ta zuba sukari ta mosa kowani kofi da dama sannan ta saurara.

Yana jira ita kuma ta jujjuya idonta.

ANNIE: ya hadu

A natse ya dauki kofin ita kuma ta kurbi nata.

ANNIE: Yaya yau Raggie?

Ya kalle ta bata saurara masa ba

ANNIE: Na ziyarci Mrs Griffihs da yamman nan a nan kusa. Naso ka kana wurin, taji dadi. Mun sha shayi da kraka kuma tayi maganganu masu dadi-saidai ta bata rai dana zuba burbudi akan bab ban kujera. Nayi fushi ita ma ta fusata,sai na…amma an gama lafiya.

Ta lurabai taba shayin shi ba tayi gyaran murya, da nufin

Ya sha.

Ya kurba kadan

ANNIE: da zaka sota. Ita kadaine…ga tsufa,kamar ka

287

Yaji abinda yake so

ANNIE: a hanyar dawa na sakararrun samarukan nan suka fara sokana na. dun saboda kullum kaya na daya duk da cewa niba kazamiyar bera bane! Sun kira ni da wadansu sunaye wanda badan fada maka ba saboda Mrs Edgley takan ce ' babu wanda zai so dyar yarinya wanda tana fadan wannan kalamun!'

tana kurban shayi kuma tana lura da fuskan shi.

ANNIE: ka kara murmushi kadan Raggie. Nan take zan gwada maka.

Ta ajiye kofin tatayi murmushi sosai.

ANNIE: (ta wutsirya) Gani? Sauran kai

Bashi da niyar murmushi sai ya harareta.

Taji bakin ciki amma taci gaba da nazartar fiskan shi.

ANNIE: Hmmm.kana jin yunwa koba haka ba?

Ya jingina

ANNIE: Kamar baka ci abincibana tsayon lokaci ba.

Taci gaba da kallon dashi.

ANNIE: na san abinda kake bukata.

Yana samani

ANNIE: Gurasa!

Ya basar.

Ta mike ta dubi kan benci-ba komai. Ba komai cikiin farantai sai idon ta yayi wasai

Ta kawo farantin kan tebur.

ANNIE: Wannan ba bin sha'awa ba!

Ta ajiye faranti a sakanin su ba komai ciki.

Da gani ya rude.

ANNIE: Nasani Raggie – ba a yanke ba tukuna. Mrs Edgley haryanzu tace nayi kankanta nayi amfani da wuka dun haka sai kayi amfani dashi.

Ta nuna masa sai taso a sanake ya shiga madafin. Ya hangi kulltun wukaken cike da wuka,ya zaro babban

Wuka mai kaifi. Ya dan saurara.

Ta zauna bisa tebur tana jefa kafafun ta kafin ya gama tana dan wake-waken ta.

Ya dawo a gajiye ya ajiye wukan a gefen faranti ya zauna. Yayi amfani da kokaran shi

Ya tura mata wuka.

Tayi mamaki

ANNIE: Da gaskiya?!

A hikimance ta dauki wukan cikin jindadi

ANNIE: Ka gani,baiwan bata yarda na samu gurasa ko yaushe. Bansan dalili ba

Watakila saboda idan na fara ci ba dan …

Da ta lura haryanzu shayin shina ajiye kan tebur sai ta bata rai.

ANNIE: Idan baka sha shayin ka ba dakaji ishi. Idan kuma kaji kishi sosai zai kawo maka rashin

Lafiya. Idan kuma ka kamu d rashin lafiya watakila ka mutu. Idan kuma ka mutu…badaka samu gurasa ba.

Bakin shi ya kadu yaja doguwar numfashi

ANNIE: bakason ka mutu ko ba haka ba?

Ta nuna masa kofin da wuka ya dauka

Da sannu yakai kofin bakin shi ya kurbi shayin.

ANNIE: Da kyau. Ga gurasan

Taje ta yanko gurasan. Ya lura da ita rike da wuka.

ANNIE: ka burge Ranka dade Reginald. Zubin mai sauki

Gwanin sha'awa. zan koyi girke-girke a wurin ka domin…

Hanun ta ya zame sai ta yanke, ta dukufa dun zafi.

Ya razana,zuciyar sa ta buga.

Yana kallo jini na kwarara a yatsar taba kakkautawa, ya bata wuri.

ANNIE:ah babu. Tayi gaskiya. Ban kai amfani da wuka ba!

Ta shiga juyayi. Kofi da yar faranti suka fara kadawa a hanun sa.

Annie na tsotse yatsar ta kuma ta lura da yanayin shi.

ANNIE: Mai ya faru? Jini. Gani?

Ta nuna masa yatsar ta yadda jini ke kwarara; yaci gaba da kwarara.

Take ya fara numfashi sama-sama sai ya sake kofi akan dabe. Ta fashe. Numfashin sa ta hau

Ga kuma tari.

Fashewan kofin yasata ta rude.

ANNIE: shike nan hakan baiyi daidai ba ko yayi?! Mrs Edgley zatayi fushi idan ta ga

Ka fasa mata tangaranta na musamman!

Ya harareta ya fusata.

Itama ta kwai-kwaye shi – ba tsoro.

Tayi salle daga kujera ta leka taga.

Dan lokuta kadan kafin su dawo hayacin su.

ANNIE: na tuba Raggie. Bana son a bata mini rai. Shi yasa nake kadaita wdansu lokuta.

Ba abin dariya bane ko?

Ta juya ta kalle shi.

ANNIE: Kadaice wa.

Ya dauke kai

Ta lashe yatsar ta sap tana jin haushi.

ANNIE: nasani baka son shayi, ko gurasa. Amma inna tunanin yana taimakawa – idan zamu zama

Abokai. Kana bukatan abota koba hakaba Raggie?

Ta kalle shi a natse amma bai kula ba.

Sai ta fiskanci taga.

ANNIE: Mrs Edgley kawata ce, na tsawon lokaci. Amma bana tunanin zan ganta

Kuma ko kuwa?

Tayi masa kollon sabo.

Ya juya a kunwace.

Ta juyo,cikin takaici ta fara zane da yatsar ta a taga.

ANNIE: Shike nan Raggie. Na saba.

290

Yayi amfani da kuzari ya tashi a hankali daga kujega.

ANNIE: idan kana son na tafi fada kawai kuma Ni dan…

TSOHO: Nikolai.

Tana haki ta juya tayi mamakin ganin shi tsaye a gaban ta.

TSOHO: sunana Nikolai.

Fiskanta ya cika da farin ciki saita wuce da rangwada.

ANNIE: Nayi farin ciki saduwa da kai, Ranka dade Nikolai.

Juyawan Annie ta lura da abu a taga ya wanda yakowo yankewan wannan yanayina farin cikin su.

ANNIE: Oh babu. Sun dawo.

Tuni yanayin damuwa ta juya zuwa tunani.

ANNIE: Damuka zama abokai yanzu, ya kamata muyi komai tare!

Saika dakata

Inna dawa.

Ta nufi kofa.

Yana yinsa ya dame ta – ya nuna baya bukatanta ta fita.

Ta dawo a sulale.

ANNIE: oh Nikolai ba masala. Inna son na gaiyace sune dun shan shayi. Akwai wadacecce

Wanda zai kai.

Tayi murmushi ta fita.

Ya damu sai ya ajiye sandar dogarawarsa akan tebur.

ANNIE: (bayan fage) kai mai katon kai! Idan ka kuskura ka shigo ka sane ni! Sai dai idan

ya kasance achikin masu razanar da kananan yan mata.

Idonsa ya wassake da sanun mafita ta rayuwa. Ya fara numfashi a sanake da tunanin samun

Gamsuwa.

ANNIE: (bayan fage wa Nikolai) Ga sunan zuwa!

Ta sake-shiga, saita masa gefe ta bawa kofa baya.

ANNIE: nayi murna da muka nemo juna Nikolai.

Ta rike hanun sa.

ANNIE: Kai ne abokin kwarai da nake dashi a cikin shekaru dari.

Tayi masa kallon kauna.

Sukayi murmushi – yana da hakori a waje.

Itama haka.

Ta kashe kendir kafin ya mutu saitaci gabada wake-waken ta.

THE CHILD NO ONE LOVES (a playlet)
By Solomon C.A. Awuzie

CHARACTERS
The Child -- the bastard
Bar Dozie -- a passerby
Odion -- a neighbour
Woman -- the child's mother
Doctor
Receptionist
people

ACT ONE

Light comes on stage. A child of about four years old squats by the road, beside him is an empty plate. People pass by him without bothering to look to his direction. As they pass him by, he raises his plate and cries out to them for help but none looks to his direction. Enter Bar. Dozie. He sees the child. He stands, observes the child for a while and then walks towards him. As soon as he is before him, the child raises the plate up to him. He looks at the child, waves his head, deepens his hand into his pocket and brings out some money. He looks at the money and then drops it into the plate.

Child: Thank you!

Bar. Dozie: What of your mother? Don't ... *(The Child stands up without saying anything. He runs across the road to buy some food with the money. Bar Dozie is dumbfounded; watches the child as he struggles to buy food for himself. Across the road is a man watching Bar Dozie from behind. Bar Dozie sees him and crosses over to meet with him.)* Hello!

Odion: Hello! How may I help you?

Bar Dozie: (forces a smile) Please, I am just curious...

Odion: curious? About what?

Bar Dozie: About that child *(points at the child).* This is not the first time I will be seeing him there. I want to know who the parents of that child are. This is because it is absurd for a parent to allow a young child like this to sit by the road all by himself, begging for alms.

Odion: That child? *(steals a glance at him and smiles)* He is on his own.

Bar Dozie: What do you mean by that? Is he an orphan?

Odion: No! He is a bastard. His mother is a whore. She attributed the child pregnancy to so many men: Portuguese, English, American, Igbo, Yoruba, Hausa so on and so forth. When she gave birth to him they all rejected him. His mother took care of him for three years and then abandoned him. Since then the child has been taking care of himself.

Bar Dozie: A child of this age taking care of himself! How? *(Enter a woman, dressed like a whore. The child is already seated, eating. She looks at the child and continue walking. Odion looks up and sees her.)*

Odion: That is the child's mother. Call her. Let's see if she would come.

Bar Dozie: (Calls her) Hello lady! (She takes a glimpse of him and continue going) Beautiful lady, I am calling you! *(She stops looks at Bar Dozie from head to his shoes and then begins to come to him.)* My name is Bar Dozie. I …

Woman: (cuts in) Please, I don't have time for stories. You know time is money. Please go straight to the point.

Bar Dozie: Please take it easy. I will pay you handsomely so don't be in a rush.

Woman: I have my prizes so please spell out what you want so that I can tell you my prize.

Bar Dozie: I want to ask you some questions …

Woman: That's no business. You want to waste my time? *(She wants to start going. He stops her again)*

Bar Dozie: I will ask you some questions and I will pay you for the time.

Woman: You will pay me three thousand naira. That is the amount I collect for shorthand.

Bar Dozie: Ok. I will pay.

Woman: Ok. Pay before service. *(Bar Dozie deepens his hand into his pocket and brings out some money. He counts three thousand naira out of the money, puts the remaining into his pocket and then gives her the three thousand naira.)*
Bar Dozie: I learnt you are the mother of that child.
Woman: (flabbergasted) Is that the question?
Bar Dozie: Yes, and I have paid for it.
Woman: Ok yes. All the men whom I supposed were responsible for his pregnancy denied him immediately after birth. They all said he does not look like them and they do not see themselves in him.
Bar Dozie: What about you? Why did you abandon him?
Woman: (upset) Why would I not abandon him? Which child looks the way he does? Tell me why a child would inherit all the bad sides of his fathers. What do you expect me to do? They all rejected him: the American hates him, the English does not like him, the Portuguese does not want him, the Igbo rejects him, the Yoruba abhors him, and the Hausa dislikes him. What do you want me to do? He was spoiling business for me so I had to leave him.
Bar Dozie: Ok I see. I will take care of him. But what is his name?
Woman: I refused to give him a name because I was not happy with him. Anyway, I was passing the other day and I heard somebody call him "Nigeria". It was funny. I stopped the person and asked him why and he said he called him that because he is always squatted by the road heading towards the River Niger and that the gutter beside him also meanders into the River Niger *(pauses and frowns).* However, if you want to take him, you can go ahead. *(pauses again)* I think your money has just expired. Thank you! *(She walks out of Bar Dozie. Bar Dozie and Odion resume their discussion in mimes. Light dims and later beams on the child as he lies by the road, shivering. Everyone continues to walk pass him without bothering to look at his direction. Bar Dozie disengages from Odion and then walks towards the child. He touches the child by his neck to know whether he is running fever.)*
Bar Dozie: (to himself) He is very sick. *(He carries the child and dashes out of platform.)*

(Snooze)

Hospital. Light beams on the doctor and nurses attending to patients. Enter Bar Dozie carrying the child. He quickly calls the doctor's attention.

Bar Dozie: Doctor! Doctor! Please this child needs urgent attention. (Doctor pays deaf ears. After a while, he turns to look at Bar Dozie.)

Doctor: You have to pay for card first.

Bar Dozie: That is not a problem. Just look at the child.

Doctor: The rule here is: you get a card first.

Bar Dozie: How much is the card?

Doctor: Please meet the receptionist.

Bar Dozie: The reception is nowhere to be found.

Doctor: You have to wait for the receptionist

Bar Dozie: Wait? Ok attend to the child. *(The doctor walks out of Bar Dozie. The child starts convulsing. Bar Dozie becomes restless. After some time enter the receptionist.)*

Receptionist: Are you the man who wants a card?

Bar Dozie: Yes! Where is the doctor? The child is convulsing. He needs to be attended to.

Receptionist: The amount is two hundred naira. *(Bar Dozie deepens his hand into his pocket and brings out two hundred naira. The receptionist collects it.)*

Bar Dozie: Please call in the doctor.

Receptionist: (feels his neck) His condition is serious. *(She dashes out of platform. After a while the child convulses again and breathes his last. Bar Dozie starts crying. A while later enter the doctor and the receptionist. He checks his eyes and his pulse.)*

Doctor: The child is dead!

Bar Dozie: Oh God! You have all killed him. You have all killed "Nigeria"!

Doctor: Who is Nigeria? Is that his name?

Bar Dozie: Yes. You have all killed him!